D1572176

Reconceiving Women's Equality in China

Reconceiving Women's Equality in China

A Critical Examination of Models of Sex Equality

Lijun Yuan

LEXINGTON BOOKS

A Division of
ROWMAN & LITTLEFIELD PUBLISHERS, INC.
Lanham • Boulder • New York • Toronto • Oxford

LEXINGTON BOOKS

A division of Rowman & Littlefield Publishers, Inc.
A wholly owned subsidiary of The Rowman & Littlefield Publishing Group, Inc.
4501 Forbes Boulevard, Suite 200
Lanham, MD 20706

PO Box 317
Oxford
OX2 9RU, UK

British Library Cataloguing in Publication Information Available

Library of Congress Cataloging-in-Publication Data

Yuan, Lijun, 1951-
  Reconceiving women's equality in China : a critical examination of models of sex
equality / Lijun Yuan.
    p. cm.
  Includes bibliographical references and index.
  ISBN 0-7391-1005-5 (hardcover : alk. paper) -- ISBN 0-7391-1228-7 (pbk. : alk. paper)
  1. Women's right--China. I. Title.
HQ1236.5.C6.Y83 2005
305.42'0951--dc22   2005008469

Printed in the United States of America

♾™ The paper used in this publication meets the minimum requirements of American
National Standard for Information Sciences—Permanence of Paper for Printed Library
Materials, ANSI/NISO Z39.48–1992.

To Boying and Shan

and to the memory of my parents

Contents

Preface

When I completed my dissertation, "Reconceiving Women's Equality in China: A Critical Examination of Models of Sex Equality," I had the strong desire to share my thoughts with all people who care about Chinese society and the situation of women in that society. I was fortunate enough to meet Robert Carley, a representative from Lexington Books, at the American Philosophical Association's Eastern Division meeting on December 28, 2003. Since then, Lexington Books has expressed interest in publishing my work. I am very impressed by the publisher, their diligent work, and their interest in bringing my book to print.

My topic is Chinese women's equality in the twentieth century. Although there were several models of sex equality to help Chinese women improve their status, the subordination of women continued under those historical forms of equality. I present a critical examination of the four models: (1) the traditional view; (2) the formal view; (3) the substantive view; and (4) equal opportunity for women's equality. I argue that in China all four failed to work in the interests of women's full equality, because they lacked a deep concern for democracy. So, in my work I provide a more democratic model of sex equality for Chinese women in the twenty-first century.

I will provide the salient details from my last chapter concerning this new model. Overall, I emphasize that the pursuits of equality and democracy are inseparable. Equality and democracy require each other. Women in China cannot achieve real equality without a new concept of the democratic pursuit of equality. This concept focuses on women's empowerment and their self-directed pursuit of equality. Two factors led me to fully engage in this project, one theoretical and the other the practicality of my own personal experiences. In the early 1990s I began to be interested in feminist philosophy and feminist interpretations of women's equality. I was primarily concerned with Chinese women's situations. In the post-Mao era, Mao's assertion that "Women can hold up half the sky" is outdated. After the Maoist era, the revival of the Confucian view of women, which encourages women to stay at home and contribute to their husbands' success rather than self-development, has increasingly become the trend. Thus, women's status has eroded, and the actual inequality between women and men in China has increased in the period of modern economic transformation. Women have been puzzled by the reality of the call for sex equality by the Chinese government, both from Mao and from post-Mao leaders. Theoretically, there was an urgent need to explore the issue of women's equality in the current climate of rapid Chinese economic development, but I saw little being done to address this explicitly in mainstream Chinese theoretical politics and Chinese feminist dialogues. Thus, I came to the University of Colorado at Boulder with the goal of learning and gaining insights from Western feminist philosophy. While I was there I decided to make my own contribution to the issue of women's equality.

The other factor that led me to this topic was my personal experience. I grew up in Mao's time and lived in the post-Mao period in China. From the end of the 1960s to the early 1970s I worked with peasant women during the Cultural Revolution. I cared very much about those peasant women's status in the great social changes after Mao died in 1976. I saw a great gap develop between urban women's and peasant women's situations in the countryside. My experiences deepened my understanding of Chinese women's diversified problems in attaining equality with men. I chose the issue of women's equality as my Ph.D. project because I cared so deeply about finding ways to help eliminate those women's oppression and subordination.

Next, I want to address how I saw my project change as I worked on it. Although I am fluent in Chinese and English and have knowledge of Chinese feminism and Western feminist thought, the topic of Chinese women's equality is still a very difficult issue. I read and studied copious materials on the issues of sex equality, but I was struck many times by the problems of gaining a clear view in my exploration of this issue. Gradually, I realized that I could not clarify this issue without a deeper investigation of democracy. So, I moved my single focus on the issue of sex equality to multiple concerns of relations between the issue of women's equality and a more democratic investment in women seeking their equality. I found these two issues closely related and necessary to the understanding of each other. This move actually reflects the insights I gained from Western feminist discourse on women's equality, especially from my advisor Alison Jaggar's recent work on issues of sex equality. Here, I see the extremely important progress made possible by the exchange of ideas between Chinese feminism and Western feminism. I am so grateful that I had this great opportunity to study Western feminist standpoints and compare them critically to the issue of Chinese women's equality. The antiessentialist thinking in Western feminism helps me greatly clarify the common problem in the old models of equality. In all of them there is a lack of emphasis on empowering women to develop their own visions of equality, while imposing top-down ideologies rationalizing women's continuing subordination. When I started to realize this common problem, I progressed smoothly to investigating the relations between democratic frameworks and women's equality.

I think I have made a great beginning for continuing the discourse on the issue of Chinese women's equality in the twenty-first century. I present a more nuanced democratic conception of equality after criticizing the nondemocratic features of the traditional four models. The point I make on this topic is crucial and clear: What Chinese women need for their equality is the empowerment of women to seek their own visions of equality, not top-down ideologies imposed on them. When Chinese women understand their own empowerment as crucial to changing their status—and the whole society together makes efforts to support women's empowerment—women will have the renewed hope of achieving full equality with men. The second important point I make regards the need for state policies favoring women, because Chinese women are too vulnerable to be competing with men in a controlled market economy. The state should not completely retreat from the market, but should help women gain equal footing by correcting the historical discrimination against them. There should be state laws protecting women's special needs, such as maternal leave, day care, and retirement. I advance a dialectical argument here: In the short term Chinese women badly need state policies to help women gain equal employment; but in the long term women should move to self-empowering programs for seeking their equality. The third point I make is a critical rethinking of the Chinese tradition of Confucianism. I hold a different view from those authoritarian defenders of Confucianism. They argue that the golden rule of reciprocity also works in women's situations, but they forget that women's three obediences would prevent them from applying reciprocity to their reality. I suggest that if the specific virtues for women, such as following men, could be transcended, then the golden rule would work to benefit women's equality.

With the above three points as my beginning, I still need to develop more details of my conception for a democratic model of equality for contemporary Chinese women. The weakness of this model at the present stage is the lack of concrete plans to empower women, especially considering problems of the feminization of agriculture, women's poverty, women's unemployment in urban districts, and the phenomenon of men keeping a second wife in highly developed cities in southern China. In a country like China, with a low material economy and a long history of patriarchal culture, it is extremely difficult to bring modern ideas of democracy and women's empowerment into practice. The democratic model for seeking women's equality requires concrete plans to empower modern Chinese women. Here, much more work needs to be done. My book is the beginning of this discourse and practice. For this, on behalf of all Chinese women, I am grateful to Lexington Books for giving me the opportunity.

Acknowledgments

I thank those who commented extensively on my work and gave enduring support to its completion. First I thank my advisor, Alison Jaggar, for encouraging me to pursue the topic of Chinese women's equality and for her incredible caring for a foreign student like me and for giving special, concrete help toward my accomplishment of this project. Her teachings about philosophy and feminist thought will inspire me through a lifetime. I thank Claudia Mills for her tremendous help in all my academic studies and for her constant support for my research work. I also thank the other members of my dissertation committee, Michael Tooley, Wes Morriston, and David Mapel, for their warmhearted support and careful attention to this project.

I owe special thanks to the graduate school at the University of Colorado for their generous support and encouragement in the form of the Graduate/Department Dissertation Fellowship and Emerson/Lowe Fellowship. Without this assistance I could not have completed this project. I thank those who helped me in various ways, including my graduate school advisor Rosella Garcia and my department secretaries, Diane Mayer, Maureen Detmer, and Olivia Carlson.

I thank my closest friends, classmates, and family for their enduring love and everyday support. Donna Reeves, Abigail Gosselin, and Theresa Weynand read and made useful comments on my early drafts, and Donna gave significant help with most chapters. Richard Jones offered crucial assistance in the final editing in preparing this book. Hye-Ryoung Kang gave me a great deal of support. Finally I thank my family, my loving parents, my husband, Boying, and daughter, Shan, for their unconditional support and love. This book is dedicated to my family.

Introduction

I came to Boulder from China in 1994 with a strong wish to learn Western feminist philosophy in the hope of gaining insights relevant to Chinese women's equality. I believe that women's status greatly improved during Mao's era (1949-1976) but has gone backwards during the last two decades. Although I know that women were devalued in Chinese traditional ethics, I am still shocked to read the news article, "Growing Sex Imbalance Shocks China."[1] Because parents are able to have a male child through selected abortion, more than 116 male births were recorded for every 100 female births, according to the results of a national census released in China in 2002. This imbalance is worsening, according to another news article, "Engineering More Sons than Daughters."[2]

Why is it that discrimination against females still persists after a century of struggle for women's equality in China? Is it because of the extreme oppressive conditions of Chinese women, exemplified in foot binding and concubinage, at the beginning of the twentieth century? Perhaps one hundred years is too short a time to catch up? Or were the various models of equality that became state policy insufficient in helping women gain equal status with men? Given the urgent need of theoretical and practical measures for women's equality in China, it is curious that Chinese feminist and mainstream theorists have made so few attempts to address this explicitly. As a philosopher, I will examine this issue through a critical discussion of Chinese traditional ideologies (Confucianism and Maoism) and several Chinese models of sex equality, some indigenous and some adopted from Western models.

I will discuss and assess four models of women's equality: first, the traditional Confucian view of women, which advocates that women's role is to follow and support men; second, the liberal feminist idea of formal equality for women introduced into China at the beginning of the twentieth century, which is anti-Confucian and advocates women's equal rights in education, law, and employment; third, Mao's view of women's equality in production, calling for substantive equality between men and women; and fourth and finally, the idea of equal opportunity in the economic transformation in the post-Mao period, the revival of Confucianism in this period, and its convergence with the declining status of women.

Each of these models has a variety of problems in dealing with women's equality, which I will discuss in the following chapters. However, I see one common thread running through all of them: namely, the lack of emphasis on empowering women to develop their own visions of equality. Ideologies imposed from the top down have rationalized the continuing subordination and exploitation of women either blatantly (in Confucianism) or more subtly (in Maoism). After exposing the common feature in their failure to reach the social ideal of women's equality, I will propose a more democratic conception of women's equality that will allow ideals to continue changing as material circumstances change in different stages of social development.

One might ask why I am qualified to undertake this project of reconceiving women's equality in China in a new century. I forward several reasons in support of my qualifications.

I was born in Beijing, China, at the beginning of Mao's time and experienced many social changes firsthand under Mao's leadership and under the post-Mao government. I was one of the millions of young people sent to rural areas to experience the hardships of peasant life during the Cultural Revolution in the 1970s. I was, however, one of the luckiest among the thousands, as I was selected to enter university and graduate school during the nation's transition to economic liberalization and an open-door policy in many fields. In addition to my personal experience as a Chinese woman living through radical social changes during the Maoist and post-Maoist periods, I was trained in Western analytic philosophy at Nankai University. I began my studies in feminist philosophy in the early 1990s, and my philosophical interest has gradually focused on issues of women's equality.

One of the most impressive practices in the recent Western feminist exploration of women's equality is the emergence of interdisciplinary efforts to support the empowerment of women: letting women speak up regarding their particular situations, rather than relying on one unified theory. This shows a more democratic direction in the exploration of women's equality. Nevertheless, Western feminist viewpoints cannot guide Chinese women's vision of equality, because they do not account for the impact of Chinese ideologies on women's situations.

Since I am fluent in Chinese and English and also have knowledge of both Chinese feminism and Western feminist thought, I can discuss dialogues and interactions between the two and examine different perspectives and models regarding women's equality. I feel confident to undertake this project because of my conversance with all the salient philosophical literature regarding this issue, on Confucianism, Marxism, Maoism, Anglo-American analytic philosophy, and feminist moral and political theory. This broad literature with its different perspectives will help me to examine models of equality with a comparative vision and to develop a democratic conception of women's equality.

My project will make contributions to several fields, including the new philosophical literature discussing Confucianism, feminist ethics and transnational feminism, democratic theory, and the new field of Chinese feminist philosophy.

I hope that my work will be utilized by the emerging Chinese women's movement and that it will make a distinct contribution to the current discussion of Chinese ideas on sexual equality.

Notes

1. John Gittings, "Growing Sex Imbalance Shocks China," *Guardian Weekly*, 16-22 May 2002.
2. Felicia R. Lee, "Engineering More Sons than Daughters," *New York Times*, 3 July 2004.

Chapter One

Confucius, Confucianism, and the Confucian Rationale for Women's Inequality

Traditional Chinese society before the twentieth century was an extremely male-dominated world. The treatment of Chinese women historically (including foot binding, concubinage, and female infanticide) was notorious around the world. No one could deny this sexism toward Chinese women (Ames and Hall 1998; Rosemont 1997; Tian 1982; Tu 1985), and some scholars believe that the oppression of Chinese women was greater than that of Western women (Ames and Hall 1998, 97). Why was it so great? Is there any connection between the traditional dominant ideology in China and the situation of women there?

Confucianism was the dominant social and moral philosophy in China for millennia. The Confucian tradition started with Confucius (551-479 B.C.). It gradually spread up through *The Analects*, edited by his disciples and followers, along with the contribution of Mencius (372-289 B.C.), as well as the *Daxue* (*Great Learning*), *Zhongyong* (*Doctrine of the Mean*), and original chapters in the *LiJi* (*Book of Rites*). Together these are called the four books and five classics of Confucian philosophy. During the Han Dynasty (206 B.C.-220 A.D.), Dong Zhong-shu (195-115 B.C.) wrote a significant work, *ChunQiu FanLu* [*Spring and Autumn Annals*], which made Confucianism the state doctrine in 136 B.C.[1] The Han rulers welcomed Confucianism as the state ideology. Dong had great influence during his time and for several hundred years, until the rise of Neo-Confucianism at the beginning of the Song Dynasty (960-1279 A.D.). Neo-Confucianism refers to a wide variety of Confucian thinkers living from the Song through the Qing Dynasties (1644-1911 A.D.). Most Neo-Confucians saw themselves as reviving, not revising, the earlier Confucian tradition. They absorbed ideas from several theories, such as Buddhism imported from India and philosophical Daoism, but insisted on keeping Confucian themes in the dominant position of the state ideology until early in the twentieth century.

Twentieth-century Chinese feminists or those concerned for women's equality sharply criticized Confucianism for justifying the extreme subordination of women. However, with the decline of Marxism and the return of capital-

ist influence, intellectuals in the Chinese diaspora and also in China have been
reviving Confucianism as an authentically Chinese ethical system that supposedly is capable of providing moral guidance during a period of rapid social
change. Feminists find Confucianism's emphasis on the importance of strong
family loyalties immediately suspect, since they know that an appeal to family
values is often a code rationalizing women's subordination. However, some
theorists argue that Confucianism is compatible with full equality for women.[2]

In this chapter I will explain the main tenets of Confucian and Neo-
Confucian thought concerning women. I will also look at several contemporary
attempts to revive Confucianism and defend it against the charge of sexism.
These different views of the Confucian stance toward women include Li Chenyang's (1994), Tu Weiming's (1985), and Ames and Hall's (1998). I will challenge these interpretations by arguing that Confucius and Neo-Confucians con-
verge in a unified line that contributes to the notion of the inferiority of women.
Nevertheless, I am open to the possibility that Confucianism might be gender-
neutral if the Threefold Obedience and Four Virtues specific for women are no
longer considered to be necessary conditions of a political environment of democracy.

Confucianism was built on the central idea of the concept of *ren* or *jen* (benevolence) and focuses on an essential ethical question: how can a human become an authentic or real person—a gentleman or an exemplary person? The
concept of *ren* has many features similar to contemporary feminist approaches
to moral thinking, such as the ethics of care (Li Chenyang 1994; Rosemont
1997). Although the Confucian concept of *ren* shares some common features
with the viewpoints of Western feminist care thinkers (the ethics of care incor-
porates the feminist pursuit of women's different moral voices), the idea of *ren*
does not seem to help women out of their oppressed situation. Instead, it encourages women to obey and to remain in their subordinated position under the will
of heaven and to accomplish their roles in accord with the harmonious orders of
a Confucian society.

There was a popular Chinese saying to express the influence of Confucian
opinions of women: "Being untalented is a virtue in a woman." This ostensible
"virtue" promoted a stereotyped notion of respectable men and humble women
in the Confucian world. Defenders of Confucianism did not investigate the connections between Confucianism and women's greater oppression, because they
did not believe such a virtue ethics practiced within the deep humanity of loving
people could lead to women's oppression. They either denied any connection
between Confucian ethical theories and the reality of women's suffering from
sexism (Tu 1985, 145), or they asserted that only Neo-Confucianism is responsible for women's oppression (Li Chenyang 1994, 85). I will present a critical
analysis of these views and explain why the virtue ethics of Confucianism promotes women's greater oppression through its insistence on virtues specific to
women. My exploration in this chapter will focus on the Confucian view of

women, starting from Confucius's *Analects,* then moving to Dong Zhong-shu's *Spring and Autumn Annals* and *The Book of Rites* and Ban Zhao's *Admonitions for Women,* and finally considering the Neo-Confucian works on women's chastity. After this historical exposition of the Confucian views of women, I will discuss whether Confucianism led to an oppressive view of women and respond to defenses of Confucianism.

The Analects

The Confucian concept of *ren* (or *jen*)[3] originated in a turbulent slave time of China called the Spring and Autumn (722-481 B.C.). Confucius lived (551-479 B.C.) in a transformational period from an early developing slave society to its decline. Facing such a revolutionary period of struggle, Confucius held a conservative political attitude, advocating the idea of overcoming oneself and restoring rituals in the Zhou (or Chou) dynasty (1111-249 B.C.). He thought that those institutions of rites in Zhou reflected various customs of respecting the old—benevolence and mercy for all—and that Zhou should be regarded as an ideal society (Li Ze-hou 1990, 2-6). Despite this, Confucius had to accept some innovations such as the abolition of the old custom of burying live slaves with their dead owners.[4] He created a doctrine of *ren* in his discourses with his disciples, and they edited those dialogues into a world-famous book, *The Analects.*[5]

In *The Analects* Confucius emphasized the idea of *ren* as humanity expressed as benevolence or universal love. This is an essence or a substantial aspect connected with the old idea of *li* (rites), the regularization of rituals in the previous Zhou society. After his death, the doctrine of *ren* was developed by later Confucians, especially those living during the Han (206 B.C.-220 A.D.) and Song (or Sung) dynasties (960-1279 A.D.). Confucianism became the dominant state ideology through the reformation of a great Confucian, Dong Zhong-shu, during the Han; later, it was consolidated through its five classics[6] and reached its summit in the Song dynasty as ritualism. The doctrine of *ren* had played a great role in the evolution of Confucianism, and radical challenges to it were barely seen publicly until early in the twentieth century, during the 1919 May Fourth Movement.

Confucius articulates the concept of *ren* as the center of his thought. The term *ren* appears more than one hundred times in *The Analects,* but the meaning of *ren* is vague and variable, and interpretations of it differ among scholars. My analysis will use the interpretations of Herbert Fingarette (1972), Feng Yu-lan (1948), Li Ze-hou (1990), and Tu Weiming (1985).[7] Among all these interpretations, the emphasis has been put on two kinds of explanations: one focusing on the man of *ren* (loving man) and the other on *ren* as overcoming oneself and restoring *li* (rite). Both of these accounts can be validated by reference to Confucius's own words. When his best disciple, Yen Yuan, asks about what *ren* is,

Confucius responds, "He who can submit himself to *li* is *jen*" (*The Analects* 12:1).[8]

What is the nature of *ren* itself? Confucius says, "A man of humanity, wishing to establish his own character, also establishes the character of others, and wishing to be prominent himself, also helps others to be prominent. To be able to judge others by what is near to ourselves may be called the method of realizing humanity" (*The Analects* 6:30).[9]

Here, *ren* is intimately linked to the relationship between men and means a reciprocal good faith and respect among men.[10] The reciprocal good faith is given a specific content: it is that set of specific social relationships articulated in detail by *li* or rites. In a word, where reciprocal good faith and respect are expressed through the specific forms defined in *li*, there is the way of *ren*. Thus, "*li* and *jen* are two aspects of the same thing" (Fingarette 1972, 42). And: "The man who really loves others is one able to perform his duties in society" (Feng 1948, 42).

According to their analysis, *ren* exists not in itself, not in speaking, but in doing, in the relationship between individual men, and in *li*. Virtues such as "loyal," "brave," and "kind" give us no insight or help in grasping the essence of *ren*, because Confucius indicates repeatedly (*The Analects* 5:18, 5:7, 14:2, 14:5) that the possession of such virtues is insufficient for establishing that a man is *ren*. For him, it is action and public circumstances that are fundamental (see Fingarette 1972, 40). Given that a man who submits himself to *li* is *ren* (*The Analects* 12:1), *ren* and *li* relate to and depend on each other. *Ren* and *li* cannot be separated in the sense that they are two aspects of the same thing. (Fingarette 1972, 42)

Every scholar who reads *The Analects* is familiar with Confucius's explanation of *ren*, namely: "To master oneself and return to propriety is humanity" (*The Analects* 12:1). This propriety refers to rites in Zhou society (1111-249 B.C.). The origin and core of rites established by customary rules in Zhou is to show great respect through sacrifices to heaven and to ancestors. These rites and customs are supposed to keep a society in good order within a hierarchical system. Significantly, the Chinese characters for the state and for the family can merge into one meaning.

The origin of "state-family" is at the starting point of Chinese history. Rulers never separated the state and the family; hence, filial piety is the first important element in *ren* structure. After the collapse of the kin and clan system, Confucius drew upon its historical traditions and turned them into a conscious ideology by emphasizing that the kinship gradation system should be kept as a universal and permanent social institution. This claim was readily acceptable to both the rulers and the ruled because of kinship's perceived biological base, which seemed to provide a naturalistic rationale for its practice, as in the customary three years' mourning for a parent's death.[11] In his book, *On the History of Ancient Chinese Thought,* Li Ze-hou gives an incisive explanation of why *li* plays an important role in performing *ren*. According to Li, Confucius explained the traditional three years' mourning period as modeled on the intimated love relationship between parents and their offspring, based on natural and psychological needs and dependencies (1990, 11-12). Thus, Confucius could explain the whole system of rituals in kin relationships in terms of the concept of filial piety and also rationalize its practices by reference to everyday loving family relations. The external or behavioral constraints of *li* were seen as stemming from the inner emotional compulsions of human needs, and so the rigid compulsory rules were promoted into the conscious idea of a good life being one combining ethical rules and psychological desires (see Li Ze-hou 1990, 12). From this model, late Confucians would easily develop a complete ethics of roles as their dominant ideology.

To Whom Was the Virtue of *Ren* Applied?

In *The Analects*, Confucius mentions women three times: First, he mentions that he visited the consort of Duke Ling of Wei, Nanzi, who was famous for both her beauty and her loose morals (6:28). Second, he said (in the case of King Wu): "With a woman amongst them [ten capable officials] there were, in fact, only nine" (8:20). Third, he claimed that women and small-minded people are hard to deal with (17:25). It is the last that has been most frequently quoted to show his attitude toward women.

Here are four alternative English translations of the Chinese original: "The master said, Women and people of low birth are very hard to deal with. If you are friendly with them, they get out of hand, and if you keep your distance, they resent it" (Waley 1938, 216-17). The second is: "In one's household, it is the women and the small men that are difficult to deal with. If you let them get too close, they become insolent. If you keep them at a distance, they complain" (Lau 1979, 148). The third is: "Women and servants are most difficult to deal with. If you are familiar with them, they cease to be humble. If you keep a distance from them, they resent it" (Chan 1963, 47). The last one is: "It is only women and morally retarded men that are difficult to raise and provide for. Drawing them close, they are immodest, and keeping them at a distance, they complain" (Ames and Hall 1998, 88).

In my own reading and understanding of this passage, I consider it important to note that Confucius's audience would agree that small men or morally retarded men and women constitute a category that is quite different from the category of gentlemen or *junzi*. Confucius has dozens of comparative sayings about the difference between the two (the term of gentleman or *junzi* in Chinese is mentioned more than one hundred times, similarly to the term of benevolence or *ren*). For instance:

4:16 "The gentleman understands what is moral. The small man understands what is profitable." 14:23 "The gentleman gets through to what is up above; the small man gets through to what is down below." 15:34 "The gentleman cannot be appreciated in small things but is acceptable in great matters. A small man is not acceptable in great matters but can be appreciated in small things." 16:8 "The gentleman stands in awe of three things. He is in awe of the Decree of Heaven. He is in awe of great men. He is in awe of the words of the sages. The small man, being ignorant of the Decree of Heaven, does not stand in awe of it. He treats great men with insolence and the words of the sages with derision." [The key of differentiating between the two is in 14:6.] "We can take it that there are cases of gentlemen who are un-benevolent, but there is no such thing as a small man who is, at the same time, benevolent." (Lau 1979, 124)

Each example places the gentleman or *junzi* higher than the small man and the gentleman as an *exemplary* model to reach *ren* or benevolence. Clearly small men as a category refers to those who are common and usually have a lower rank in society. According to Confucius, a small man is a morally retarded person, and so is a woman. Confucius excludes women from the discussion of how to reach a high level of being benevolent: "The common people, insofar as they make no effort to study even after having been vexed by difficulties, are the lowest" (16:9). Nothing that Confucius says presenting *ren* as a perfect virtue has any application to women and small men in *The Analects*. To Confucius, only the elite scholars like *junzi* can realize his idealistic model of *ren,* and they must be highly self-cultivated men. Women were too low even to aspire to the high standard of moral state he imagined, and he excluded them from his discussions of *ren* in *The Analects*.

The idea of *ren* is similar to the idea of self-cultivation. Being self-cultivated is synonymous with taking joy in learning and being a real person or a *junzi*. A *junzi* means an elite, noble, and profoundly moral person. A *junzi* must be a model of *ren*, an exemplary man. The way to be a *junzi* is not by birth but by self-cultivation, a lifelong process of learning and becoming. Through great learning and love of learning, people would promote their characters and keep their proper names and identities. Therefore, the whole world and society would be in a harmonious order and prosperous. This is expressed in Confucius's famous passage (12:11): "Let the ruler be a ruler, the subject a subject, the father a father, the son a son." A father who does not act as a father ought not be called "father." A ruler who does not act as a ruler is not deserving of the name. This doctrine of Zhengming (the proper use of names) elicited tremendous influence in Chinese society both on rulers and ruled. Although there is no mention of women in this passage, thinking by analogy suggests that the mother must be a mother, the daughter a daughter, and the wife a wife. This implication was emphasized in late Confucianism and Neo-Confucianism.

Yin-Yang Confucianism in *Spring and Autumn Annals*

Dong Zhong-shu (or Tung Chung-shu, 179-104 B.C.) was the greatest Confucian of his time and for several hundred years afterward. He established Neo-Confucianism with his famous doctrine of Yin-Yang and Five Agents, which were embedded in a complete cosmological pattern called the correspondence of man and Heaven. Dong played a crucial role in transferring Confucianism into the dominant state ideology while abolishing a hundred schools of other ideologies during the Han dynasty (see Feng Yu-lan 1948, 191).

What Dong did at that time provided a theoretical ground for the new social and political orders under the rule of Han emperors. According to him, the foundation of human actions should be found in Heaven (by heaven he means the combination of God and nature; see Feng Yu-lan 1948, 192), since humans are part of Heaven. He adopted the thoughts of yin-yang that appeared in necromancers' explanation about nature and human affairs in the pre-Chin period (255-221 B.C.), and he thought there were close relationships between humans and the Heavens. Based on this assumption, he combined the original yin-yang doctrines as the grounds of metaphysics with his Confucian social and political philosophy.

In *A Source Book in Chinese Philosophy,* Chan gives a concise explanation of yin-yang doctrines:

> In simple terms, the doctrine teaches that all things and events are the products of two elements, forces, or principles: yin, which is negative, passive, weak, and destructive, and yang, which is positive, active, and constructive. The theory is associated with that of the Five Agents or Elements (Wu-hsing refers to Metal, Wood, Water, Fire, and Earth), which may be taken as an elaboration of the yin-yang idea, but actually adds the important concept of rotation, i.e., that things succeed one another as the Five Agents take their turns. (1963, 244)

In yin-yang doctrines, the universe is conceived of as a well-coordinated system in which everything is related to everything else. With this idea, Dong transformed Confucianism. His interpretation of Confucianism became the ruling ideology of the Chinese emperors. In Dong's interpretation of the Five Agents, he put an order to them: The first is Wood; the second, Fire; the third, Earth; the fourth, Metal; and the fifth, Water. Wood is the beginning of the cycle of the Five Agents, Water is its end, and Earth is its center. Such is their natural sequence (Chan 1963, 279).

Such is their order as that of father and son. It is the way of Heaven that the son always serves his father, and Earth serves Heaven with the utmost loyalty. Therefore, the Five Agents are the actions of filial sons and loyal ministers. Unlike the yin-yang school, which puts the Five Agents in a cycle, Dong arranges them lineally, in a straight-line sequence. In human relations, the hierarchy becomes three *kangs* or bonds to keep the great order. Like Fire enjoying Wood, the function of the son is to receive and to fulfill; like Water overcoming Metal, one should bury one's father in three years' mourning; like Earth showing respect to Heaven, serving the ruler must be done with the utmost loyalty.

Dong's main views and philosophy are included in the book *Spring and Autumn Annals (ChunQiu FanLu).*[12] According to Dong's interpretation, Heaven would allow yang to develop as he likes, but would not allow yin to do so. Also Heaven would prefer goodness and kindness to evil and punishment (see Feng 1948, 194). Since yin-yang doctrines can be accepted as a metaphysical ground for justifying social orders, Dong developed these thoughts into Yin-Yang Confucianism. Dong said:

> In all things there must be correlates. Thus if there is the upper, there must be the lower. If there is the left, there must be the right. If there is cold, there must be heat. If there is day, there must be night. These are all correlates. The Yin is the correlate of the Yang, the wife of the husband, the subject of the sovereign. There is nothing that does not have a correlate, and in each correlation there is the Yin and Yang. Thus the relationships between sovereign and subject, father and son, and husband and wife, are all derived from the principles of the Yin and Yang. The sovereign is Yang, the subject is Yin; the father is Yang, the son is Yin; the husband is Yang, the wife is Yin. The three cords [*Kang*] of the Way of the [true] King may be sought in Heaven." (in Feng 1948, 196-97)

According to Dong, the Three *Kangs* (the ruler, the father, and the husband) are to be the standards of the ruled, the son, and the wife. *Kang* means principles or bonds, literally "the big ropes." All of the smaller ropes should connect with the big ropes and obey them as inferiors (Feng 1948, 196-97). Besides the Three *Kangs*, Dong also advocates the Five Norms (Humanity, Obligation, Rites, Wisdom, and Faith). According to Dong, Confucius understood the origin of things and the way of Heaven, and he taught humanity (*ren*) and righteousness, rooted in Heaven. Thus, the final power of interpreting what is correct or not rests with Confucian scholars. The Three *Kangs* as social ethics and the Five Norms as individual virtues are combined together into one moral law, which was established as the root of Chinese culture and civilization (Feng 1948, 197).

Unlike Mencius[13] who claimed that goodness is in all humans, Dong created a classification of three types of men. Dong emphasizes the relation between name and realization. All men are named by goodness but cannot come into truth without instruction. To him, every man has the beginning of goodness in his nature, which also involves evil. The highest type not only has the beginning but almost goodness in his activity, and the lowest type has almost no beginning at all (see Chan 1963, 276). Goodness in ordinary people, according to his view, differs fundamentally from goodness in a sage (see Huang Pumin 1992, 149). Thus, Dong anticipates three grades of human nature and provides a base for his doctrine of a King governing and endowed by Heaven (see Feng 1948, 198). As the founder of state Confucianism, Dong played a significant role in inhering the original Confucian ideas (originating with Confucius and Mencius), and most importantly, in transforming Confucian thought, in particular the thought of governing the state with *li* (the order of hierarchy), into the only dominant ideology among many other views of politics and moral thinking.

The unity of Chinese society in Qin (221-206 B.C.) and Han (206 B.C.-220 A.D.) provided the soil for a dominant ideology like Dong's state Confucianism, and it was so welcomed by these rulers and following emperors that it became a symbol of Chinese tradition. Yin-Yang and the Five Agents became the pattern of being harmonious, stable, and balanced. Confucianism and great unity became the foundation of Dong's ideology.

Although Dong did not specifically focus on a view of women's inferiority, his main point of the Three *Kangs* and the governing of *li* set up a main tenet of the Confucian view of women. According to Yin-Yang Confucianism, women should always be subject to their men since yin should always correlate to yang and not be allowed to develop itself independently. The justification of women's inferiority in this theory encouraged other Confucian classics like *The Book of Rites* (*LiJi*), *Admonitions for Women* (*NuJie*), etc., to present a rationale for women's oppression.

LiJi, NuJie, and *QiChu*

Originally, *LiJi* was only a number of Confucian jottings, but during the Han and Tang dynasties they gradually grew into a book, a classical Confucian text. Eventually, its position rose to become one of the five classics in state scholarship. A chapter called *LiYun* (*The Evolution of Rites*) in *LiJi* expresses the final stage of social progress according to Confucian idealism: "When the great Tao was in practice, the world was common to all; men of talents, virtue, and ability were selected; sincerity was emphasized and friendship was cultivated . . . Kindness and compassion were shown to widows, orphans, childless men, and those who were disabled by disease, so that they all had the wherewithal for support. Men had their proper work and women had their homes. This was called the great unity" (quoted in Feng 1948, 203). This great unity, peace, and order, presenting people's dreams, could be easily used by rulers to serve their own purpose of stabilizing the unification of the empire, which the Qin dynasty had first achieved in 221 B.C.

Since the ritual of spouses was considered to be one of the most important things in following the way of yin and yang, *LiJi* set up various regulations for practicing rites—and, in particular, rites for women to follow. Why should people learn and practice those complicated and tedious formalities? The first chapter called *QuLi* explains this by separating humans and other animals: every one knows he or she is not a beast since humans act with the rules of rites. Thus, the ritualization of human society is the only difference between humans and wild animals. By this separation of humans and beasts through rites, the Confucian teaching of rites sounds very natural and acceptable; therefore, it is easy for people to follow and practice. Many subtle regulations such as the male and female do not touch hands, do not sit at the same table, do not communicate with each other before being married, etc., (Li Jun 1980, 776-84) became very influential in Chinese society for two thousand years. There is no doubt that the popularity of arranged marriage came from and was encouraged by the tradition of these rites.

Regulations within marriage seemed more favorable to yang than to yin as written in chapter *NeiZe* (*Domestic Regulations*) in *LiJi*. The most famous passage in *LiJi* is as follows: "Woman following man is the beginning of the correct relation between husband and wife; obedience to the father before marriage, to the husband after marriage, and to the son after the husband's death" (Li Jun 1980, 1003). These are the principles of Threefold Obedience—a specific virtue for women but not for the elite and ordinary men.

Following *LiJi*, Ban Zhao, in the late Han, wrote *NuJie* (*Admonitions for Women*, edited by Zhang, 1996). *LiJi and NuJie* became the canonical authority for later literature of moral instruction that expressed a systematic ethical theory of engendered virtues. *NuJie* has seven short chapters:

(1) Petty, low, and fragile first
(2) Rituals between husband and wife
(3) Respect and caution
(4) Four virtues of women (loyalty, proper speech, modest demeanor,
     and diligent work)
(5) Single-hearted devotion
(6) Obedience to all
(7) Kindness to husband's siblings

All of these advise women to understand that to be inferior is to submit to all family members: parents-in-law, husband, husband's siblings, and sons. A woman should subordinate herself completely to the family she marries into without any preoccupation for herself. In the beginning of chapter 5, Ban Zhao says: "According to *LiJi*, a husband can marry others or have concubines to fulfill his obligations to the family, but a wife cannot marry again. Therefore, her husband is her Heaven" (1996, 3). The husband is the Heaven for the wife: the wife can never leave her husband except when he refuses her, since she must obey the will of the Heaven. The only way for a wife to avoid the fate of abandonment is to serve her husband and his family wholeheartedly and in accord with those admonitions. If those admonitions provide positive persuasions for women to follow, they also provide negative excuses for men to abandon them no matter how hard women might have tried in their service to the family-in-law. Men could cite any one of seven reasons to justify abandonment of their wives (*QiChu*) and such abandonment would put women into the most miserable situations.

In *Discourse on the History of Chinese Women's Life* (Tian 1982), divorce is called "refused marriage." For women, to divorce was to be forced to leave, but for husbands, it was to give up their wives. According to folk sayings, there were at least seven reasons or excuses for abandoning a wife (*QiChu*):

(1) Failing to obey the father- and mother-in-law
(2) Failing to give birth to a male descendant
(3) Sexual relations with others than the husband
(4) Envy for the husband's concubines
(5) Serious disease and loss of the ability to serve the family
(6) Gossip
(7) Stealing the family's possessions.
(Quoted in All China Women's Federation 1981, 164-69)

These reasons for abandoning a wife became the man's absolute privilege. Hence, from the master Confucius[14] in the Spring and Autumn period (722-481 B.C.) to the elite and ordinary people in the Han, Song, Ming, and Qing dynasties, to abandon a wife seemed a trivial decision. The rules of Seven *Chu* were adopted as a foundation of law in the Han dynasty (Tian 1982, 50). It was no surprise to hear a popular folk saying: "To be a person, one should never wish to be a female, because, all her life, pleasure and pain would be controlled by others" (49).

One objection could be that men seemed not to be so free to abandon their wives without parental agreement. Men did things as their parents wished in order to be a Xiaozi (a son of filial piety). Nevertheless, men still had options to get another wife or more concubines, but the wife had no weapons to fight against the decision of abandonment. Women were always vulnerable in family relations and there were tremendous restrictions on their actions, according to *LiJi, NuJie,* and *QiChu.*

Neo-Confucian View of Women

The situation of women after the Song dynasty (960-1279 A.D.) became worse since Neo-Confucianism emerged in a prosperous age of recovery following a period of confusion during the Five Dynasties after the collapse of the Tan (618-907 A.D.). Cheng-Zhu Li Xue[15] was the most prominent school carrying on the Confucian tradition with a focus on women's special virtues and chastity. I will describe Zhu Xi's and the two Chengs' views of women in this section.

Zhu Xi (or Chu His, 1130-1200 A.D.) was one of the greatest Confucians of his time. He has exercised great influence on Chinese thought since the Song dynasty. He gave Confucianism new meaning and for centuries dominated the thought of China and her neighboring countries. One of Zhu's important doctrines is "the moon is everywhere visible." He holds an idea of a Supreme Ultimate, which is more mystical than Plato's idea of the Good or Aristotle's God (see Feng 1948, 298). According to his analysis, each individual can receive a Supreme Ultimate in its entirety, just like the moon shining in the sky, reflected in rivers and lakes. We can see the moon everywhere and would not say it is divided. This principle in the universe shows us its eternity without beginning or end. There are two fundamentals of the universe: Yin and Yang. The interaction of the Yin and Yang results in the production of the Five Elements, and from these elements the physical universe is produced. When this concept is applied to Zhu's ethical and political philosophy, it implies that the *Tao* of Heaven decides the destiny of the ruler and the ruled (Feng 1948, 303).

As for destiny, Zhu was once asked if Yin and Yang should be equal and, therefore, the number of worthy and unworthy people should be equal. Why is it that there are always fewer superior men and more inferior men? He said:

> Naturally things and events are confused and mixed. How can they be equal? If there were only a single yin and a single yang, everything would be equal. But because of the great complexity and infinite transformation of things, it is impossible to have everything just right. The mere fact is that whenever the courses of material force reach a certain point and meet, a sage or a worthy is born. After he is born, it does seem that Heaven had such an intention. (Chan 1963, 627)

All his answers seem to focus on predestination and conformity to the *Tao* of Heaven. Under Zhu's principle of Heaven and universal loving with difference and gradation, women are in the lowest position and the most unworthy and least cared about. The words of a famous scholar, Cheng Yi (Cheng I), show women's status: "A widow dying of hunger was a matter of little account, but remarriage, which would desecrate her chastity, was a serious matter." To practice such martyrdom (starving to death or committing suicide before being raped) had become an increasingly popular custom (Chow 1994, 208-10).

Many works of the Cheng-Zhu school were in varying degrees inspired by Zhu's books: one called *Family Rituals*, the other an unfinished study, *A General Exposition of the Classic and Commentaries on the Book of Etiquette and Decorum*. These ritual studies inevitably influenced the social guides of popular norms. As Kai-wing Chow says in his book, *The Rise of Confucian Ritualism in Late Imperial China*, "The *Family Rituals* stimulated both ritual practices and ritual scholarship and served as a primer for gentry attempts to establish family rituals" (Chow 1994, 135). Many proponents of the Cheng-Zhu school fully endorsed widow and fiancée chastity. They argued that chastity on the part of a betrothed maiden was commendably in accord with the rules of propriety. Dai Zhen (Tai Chen)[16] commented: "Widows who refused to remarry and were willing to bear the wretched consequences of widowhood, including death, had attained the highest virtues of humanity (*ren*) and duty (*yi*)" (quoted in Chow 1994, 210). This claim encouraged an increasingly popular custom of practicing such martyrdom, as Chow points out in the following.

> The dramatic increase in the member of chaste widows owed much to a change in the criteria for award. Since 1304 honorific insignia had been granted chaste widows who were over 50 and had been under 30 when their husbands died. In 1723, the minimum age for the award was reduced to 40 and the required period of chastity to 15 years. In the early nineteenth century, widows who had remained unmarried for 10 years qualified for honorific insignia. Another factor in the rapid increase in the number of faithful widows was the government's practice of seeking out women from poor families whose virtues would otherwise have remained unrecognized. (Chow 1994, 208)

By Chow's observation, widows might wish to remain chaste for two reasons. First, a widow could, in the name of remaining faithful to her deceased husband, resist attempts to put her on the market as a concubine. Second, she could utilize the custom of patrilineage to maintain and enhance her status as a head of her own household. Chastity became a means for a woman to survive. If it were a virtue according to the rationalistic school, "It had become such a sacred virtue that voluntary and forced suicides were committed in its name" (1994, 212).

Obviously, chastity was a test of loyalty for women, yet it was never expected of men. Widows and fiancées were expected to remain chaste when their husbands or fiancées died, while husbands could have as many concubines as they could afford. As we have seen, it was popular and acceptable to society for a gentleman to buy more concubines after he married his wife, but his wife could never leave him and remarry. Also accepted was the custom of foot binding of women, to bind their feet in order to satisfy men's taste in beauty. (A properly bound foot was called a three-inch golden lotus.).

As we see, great Confucian masters like Dong and Zhu agreed with Confucius that the concept of *ren* cannot be understood apart from that of *li*, for *li* represents *ren* in its particular acts, and emphasizes ritualism as the most important aspect of *ren*. The prominent position of rites in Confucianism became increasingly crucial to consolidating the feudal and autocratic system of Chinese society, in particular, as a useful tool to oppress women.

What remains common between Confucius and later Confucianism is the implication of *ren*: love with gradation. People were born into stratification. Their biological identities determined their social ranks. A sage or a sovereign was sent from Heaven; hence, a sage deserved the highest respect and love. But a petty man and a woman supposedly did not deserve equal respect, love, or caring as higher people did. This theory was welcomed by all rulers in Chinese feudal society and was adopted as the state ideology for almost two thousand years. Only when Western science and democracy were introduced into China in the late nineteenth and early twentieth century, especially during the May Fourth Movement from 1917 to 1919, did the old unshakable standing of Confucianism begin to crumble.

Comments on Different Perspectives on the Confucian View of Women

Having exposed the Confucian view of women through *The Analects*, the *Spring and Autumn Annals*, *LiJi*, *NuJie*, and Cheng-Zhu, I wish to move now to discuss several contemporary scholars' thoughts on the Confucian view of women. Since those primary Confucian texts do not deal with the feminist issue of women's equality, but only with how women fit into the hierarchy of Confucian society, I will not directly relate those texts with current feminist discussion of women's issues. Instead, I will focus on contemporary interpretations of the Confucian view of women and assess their claim that feminism and Confucianism are compatible. It is crucial to clarify this relationship for Chinese women and other people who support the social ideal of women's equality. I have chosen Li Chenyang, Tu Weiming, and Roger Ames and David Hall as the contemporary interpreters of the Confucian view of women since they are sympathetic to contemporary ethics of care and feminist thinking about selfhood.

Tu is a world-renowned expert in Confucian humanism as a living tradition; Li is an active scholar in comparative study between the Confucian concept of *ren* and feminist ethics of care (Li Chenyang 1994, 1999, and 2000); Ames and Hall, as American scholars of Chinese philosophy, contribute to the assessment of Confucian traditional thought in light of contemporary Western moral thinking, including feminist ethics. All of these scholars stand as experts on Confucianism, and they claim that the Confucian view of women is authentic Chinese ethics and does not necessarily justify women's oppression. I find that their interpretations of the Confucian view of women are very stimulating, but as a woman philosopher with personal experiences of the Anti-Confucian movement in the Cultural Revolution (1966-1976) of Mao's time, I hold a different perspective from the above scholars on the political significance of the Confucian tradition for women. Based on these different perspectives, I will analyze Li's and Tu's interpretations of the Confucian view of women in this section and will turn to Ames and Hall, and my own view, in the next section.

Chenyang Li[17] denies any connections between Confucius's view of women and the Neo-Confucian view of women, and he claims that only later Confucians such as Dong and Neo-Confucians such as Cheng-Zhu should be held responsible for women's oppression (see Li Chenyang 1994), not Confucius and Mencius. The argument he gives to support this claim is the similarity of Confucius's concept of *ren* to the feminist ethics of care: love with gradations in a particular situation. I wrote an article (2002) examining this argument and countering that feminist ethics is different from the concept of *ren*. The former aims to eliminate women's subordination. In the sense of a feminist goal, the concept of *ren* is not helpful to women because it is not applicable to women's situation. The category of women, just like the category of small men in *The Analects*, is different from the category of *junzi* (gentlemen). Women simply do not count in Confucius's mind.

To the question of whether Confucius made contributions to the idea of women's inferiority or not, my answer is yes. Confucius indicated the main line of the Confucian view of women in his *Analects,* and his followers did not misunderstand his point: women were born with a lower identity that was unchangeable in Chinese history. We can see that the difference between Confucius and later Confucians in their attitudes toward women consists in their different strategies: exclusion of women in *The Analects* or inclusion in Neo-Confucian works focusing on chastity. Yet they never truly considered women as respectable as men because women were a second sex in all those admonitions of Confucian literatures such as *LiJi, NuJie,* and Zhu's unfinished book *Family Rituals.*

In my view, love, or care, is wonderful for every person. If this love is a kind of universal love and not peculiar to one sex, as Li argues, it should not be true that women deserve less love or care because of their sex. The deep inegalitarianism of Confucius and Confucianism inevitably resulted in oppressive views of women. These views consistently matched each other on the issues of women, either by excluding women in the application of *ren* in Confucius, or by including women with their special virtues of being subordinate in later Confucianism.

The second defense of Confucianism is from Weiming Tu.[18] He differs with Li about Neo-Confucianism in the Song dynasty, and he argues that the notion of *ren* in Neo-Confucianism does not lead to women's oppression because it is sexually neutral, and *ren* is a general virtue for all people (Tu 1985). This view tries to tell us that empirical gender norms are irrelevant in a discussion of ethical theory. Nevertheless, this so-called gender-neutrality was not true in the practical implications of both Confucius and Confucianism, as I previously argued.

Tu describes *ren* (*jen*) "as a living metaphor," which is compatible with his explanation of Confucius's concept of selfhood. He focuses on the Neo-Confucian's contribution to the concept of self, which entails a continuous enlargement of the self. As for the Neo-Confucian position on the role of women, Tu argues that women, like men, actively shape their own moral character. The task of learning to be human involves "a dynamic process of growth rather than mere submission to assigned social roles" (Tu 1985, 144). According to this viewpoint, the Neo-Confucian masters hold the universalistic claim that every human being, in the sense of the sexually neutral form of *ren*, has the potential to form a unity with Heaven, Earth, and myriad things. Tu's argument suggests that Neo-Confucians did not prescribe any practices of excluding women from highly moral self-realization.

Although Tu agrees with the idea that China was unquestionably a male-dominated society, he denies any connections between women's oppression and Neo-Confucian ethics. He thinks that Neo-Confucians hold that the governing virtue between husband and wife is based not only on the idea of the division of labor but also on the value of mutual appreciation or respect. The idea of mutual respect based on the principle of reciprocity leads Tu to argue that a wife-mother, just like a husband-father, could also function creatively at each stage of her self-realization. She realized herself through the "procedural freedom" that she cultivated despite her structural limitation (Tu 1985, 144).

This argument receives a challenge from Margery Wolf in "Beyond the Patrilineal Self."[19] Through the investigation of shaping the self in the family, Wolf argues that the male-dominated family is the context within which the self is formed and the adult self is measured; hence, sex really matters in shaping the self. This challenge supports my doubt that Neo-Confucianism allows a woman, like a man, to creatively achieve her self-realization, as Tu believes. There have been a few exceptions in the long history of Chinese society, such as Ban Zhao, who could realize self-fulfillment as a gentleman could, but she is an exception to what she advocated in her *Admonitions for Women*: "Lack of talent is a virtue in a woman." (Being untalented is a virtue for women.)

Hence, whether a woman in the Confucian world could reach self-realization as a man could seems unlikely. Furthermore, Ban Zhao came from a high-ranking family and had economic advantages to develop her talents. Women of lower-class families would not have the same opportunities to shape their selves in their specific situations. Thus, Tu's argument of universal moral self-realization cannot be true in regard to different women's contexts.

Self-transformation and self-realization, I believe, have at least two presuppositions: self-knowledge and self-determination (self-goverment). These, however, also demand a good education and time to learn. Confucianism's three dependencies (Threefold Obedience) usually prevented women from gaining these opportunities. Chinese families typically prioritized the boys' education and were unwilling to pay for a girl's education. Lacking the ability of self-knowledge and self-governing, a woman could rarely realize anything she wished. In every decision she made, she had to consult with her father, husband, or son. In the male-centered culture, a woman could only adjust herself to fit the existing social norms and customs that were supporting this patriarchal society.

How could a woman creatively realize herself if she had to learn from the very beginning (as a little girl) to serve others at home without a concern for herself?

The Neo-Confucian masters like Cheng-Zhu in the Song dynasty did insist that respect and mutual appreciation should be valued in the relationship between women and men, and they did encourage women's participation in shaping the form of human relations in the family. Zhu encouraged education for women within the proper limits of moral tracts and directions toward the proper goals of women assisting their husbands. He articulated what was to become a standard position on women by saying, "A wife submits herself to the will of another; her rectitude consists of not following her own will" (Zhu Xi's *Elementary Learning* XX 2:35, quoted in Raphals 1998, 255). However, at best, Zhu's instruction means that women only would be conscientiously perfecting and participating in shaping their roles of subordination. The conscientious efforts in shaping moral character have significant influence on women's views about their own destiny, which is conforming to the idea that a woman is born for the service of man.

The Neo-Confucian masters encouraged women to adjust themselves into virtuous women through their ultimate self-transformation. Cheng Yi showed this idea in his famous claim, "A widow dying of hunger was a matter of little account, but remarriage, which would desecrate her chastity, was a serious matter." In Cheng's mind, perhaps the total commitment to the sacredness of marriage could be applied equally to husband and wife. But in practice, a husband could have concubines when his wife was alive, and his wife could lose her integrity by remarrying after her husband died. Furthermore, in Cheng's theory, the true meaning of matrimony was not simply economic need, or romantic love, but rather mutual responsibility. The wife and husband should treat each other with full respect. But the wife should conduct herself with humility and obedience. According to Confucian logic, reciprocal respect and mutual responsibility have different meanings for the mother and father, the wife and husband.

The division of labor between the inner (domestic) and the outer (public) spheres of responsibility makes it necessary for a wife to play a major role at home. A good wife should prefer consulting her husband even in small matters, because she has no right to make independent decisions. Her position of obedience keeps her continuously adjusting herself to fit her roles; only when passive acceptance of her fate has changed into positive participation in shaping those roles can she reach ultimate self-realization.

A virtuous woman without any talents would be a perfect model of women's social roles in the Neo-Confucian text. A conscientious woman with a deep faith in Neo-Confucian ideology would earnestly teach and train women in the roles of subordination so that they could become fully human in the Confucian world. This can be illustrated by the fact that it was women themselves who forced their daughters to be foot-bound. A virtuous woman should assist her husband to have concubines in order to keep the male family line strong in the Confucian society.

Under the influence of Song and Ming Neo-Confucianism, a wide variety of those texts of instruction were reinterpreted to reinforce earlier inflexible formulations of women's virtues. Women were encouraged to learn and to participate in transforming themselves to follow the Confucian emphasis on women's chastity and specific virtues (Raphals 1998, 254). Obviously, these specific moral requirements for women expressed the rationale of Confucian culture for women's inferiority. Neo-Confucian ideology significantly contributed to the indoctrination of women into voluntary subordination during that period.

On "Correlative Sexism"

The third defense of Confucianism is from Roger T. Ames[20] and David L. Hall (1998, 1999). They argue that from China's classical beginnings as seen in *The Analects* to the present, Chinese society has been and still is male-dominated and sexist. Nevertheless, China's sexism is different from Western dualistic sexism (1998, 89). The point they try to make is that the understanding of gender-construction in China is quite different from that prevailing in Western societies. Henry Rosemont also holds a similar viewpoint about Chinese gender structure (see 1997, 68). Ames and Hall claim that the particular forms of sexism in the West were culturally entrenched and could not be fundamentally resolved without a radical philosophical revolution (Ames and Hall 1998, 87). The cosmological contrasts in the Western tradition have tended toward exclusive dualism; however, those in China tended toward complementary pairings (82). The basic polarity in China will doubtless involve the mutually implicated contrasts (light and dark, active and receptive, etc.). The basic polarity in the West will involve mutually inconsistent pairings. According to these understandings, Chinese culture based on Confucian and Daoist (Taoist) philosophy has been strongly colored by feminine gender characteristics (85). Yet, they claim, Chinese philosophy has been no less a male-dominated occupation than Western philosophy. Hence, "There seems to be something more fundamental than gender difference at issue" (85).

When Ames and Hall explain "correlative sexism," they use Daoism rather than Confucianism. In Chinese culture, heart-and-mind (xin) makes emotion and rationality co-present and inseparable. The same is true of yin-yang gender traits. Dao pursues balance and harmony, and when this is upset, it works to restore it. Similarly, the *Daodejing* (the first classic of Daoism, written by Laozi) embraces yin characteristics as an appropriate antidote for the imbalance in the human world. "The *Daodejing* is not advocating the substitution of yin values for the prevailing yang ones. On the political level, the *Daodejing* is not advocating the application of yin-based techniques to achieve the yang-inspired end of political control. Rather, the text pursues both the personal and the political ideal that reconciles the tension of opposites in sustained equilibrium and harmony." It would seem to imply the interdependence of opposites and their reconciliation through an achieved harmony and balance that recognizes "the value of difference" (Ames and Hall 1998, 93).

Ames and Hall give a further explanation on the Confucian side: neither human nature nor gender is a given, according to Confucian ethics. "A person is not born a woman, but becomes one in practice. And gender identity is ultimately not one of kind, but resemblance. The sexist problem, then, will be one of degrees of disparity rather than strict inequality" (1998, 95-96). So, males and females are created as a function of difference in emphasis rather than difference in kind. Within the correlative model, the richest correlations are those that stand in the greatest degree of contrast.

> Hence, equality defined in terms of univocity and sameness is a casualty of difference and diversity. At the same time aesthetic coherence demands that there be centers that draw differences into harmony and have implicate within them a sense of a broader field. Corollary to difference then is the necessity of hierarchy. (Ames and Hall 1998, 96)

In this passage, Ames and Hall are trying to unify Daoist and Confucian versions of gender complements rather than dichotomous relations. However, it is not clear how they could draw the necessity of hierarchy from their correlative model of gender relations in Daoism. It seems that they see the aesthetic coherence in that model demands differences of functions to form harmonious order, and they draw the necessity of hierarchy from those differences. Nonetheless, it seems those differences of functions in different roles performed by people only entail a hierarchy of functions but not a hierarchy of gender. They did not move to this point, but stopped on hierarchy.

In spite of those features in the correlative model, Ames and Hall note that the problem of sexism is likely as great, or even greater, in China than in industrialized Western societies. Why is it greater? According to their discussion, "The correlative model is more fluid and less stable than the dualistic one. The flexibility that permits a greater degree of creativity in the correlative model also permits a greater degree of abuse and grosser violations of human dignity" (Ames and Hall 1998, 97).

This point of flexibility sounds very insightful. On the other hand, the authors fail to explain why this model led to the greater abuse of Chinese women in the past, and I have some reservations about their suggestion. My response to their analysis of "correlative sexism" is the following.

First, there is a contrast in Daoist and Confucian views of correlative things such as yin-yang, sun-moon, strong or weak (soft), etc. Daoism definitely favors yin, the moon, and soft, while Confucianism prefers yang, the sun, and strong.

In a word, the hierarchy is more important as an aim to justify the harmony of human relations in Confucian views of gender roles. There is a big jump from differences of functions in gender roles to differences of persons in their gender roles, a jump from a hierarchy of gender roles into a hierarchy of different genders. This analysis is missing in their discussion. It would not be correct to consider sexism as rooted in Daoism and to argue that the Daoist pursuit of correlative pairs is the model of correlative sexism, because Daoist thinking is a correlative model but not typical sexism. The charge of sexism should belong to the Confucian view of women rather than to the Daoist view of women.

According to Feng, the main sources of Neo-Confucianism came from three lines of thought: "The first, of course, is Confucianism itself. The second is Buddhism, together with Taoism via the medium of Ch'anism. Finally, the third is the Taoist religion, of which the cosmological views of the Yin-Yang School formed an important element" (Feng 1948, 268).

These three lines of thought were heterogeneous and even in many respects contradictory in their original themes. Confucians did not unify the heterogeneous features of the three. Confucianism became the authoritarian scholarship and was reaffirmed as the official teaching of the state when the Emperor Tai-Zong commended it to be taught in the Imperial University in 630 A.D. (see Feng, 266). It took a long time during their competition with the strong rivals of Chan Buddhism and Daoism for the Neo-Confucian philosophers to unify these three lines of thought, and these scholars turned these three philosophies into "a genuine system forming a homogeneous whole" (269). In this homogeneous whole, hierarchy was the necessity, and harmonious relations between gradations of people meant a cooperation of different positions but not a diversity of equal concern.

Second, Ames and Hall argue that in the correlative model, the culturally stipulated differences in function stimulate interdependence between the male and female that is cumulative, and this ideally promotes mutual interest, need, and affection. To the contrary, I would doubt this notion of mutual interest when looking at how those threefold obedience, and four virtues for women affected a woman's life. A woman's interest was supposedly included in the unit of the family rather than in herself.

Yet, this totally neglects the situation of family abuse of women and assumes that the male head of the family would not benefit more from the domination of women. It seems to me this correlative sexism could cover sexist essence by emphasizing its mutual interests, needs, and affection. According to Cheng-Zhu instruction, a wife must submit herself to the will of a husband; if that is the case, how can the mutualization be true to women? The so-called mutualization and correlations were true only at the lower level of cohabitation but not at the level of decision-making or equal respect. This mutual interest meant, in a family of one husband and more than one wife or concubine, that it applied differently to different genders: strict monogamy for women but polygamy for men.

The custom that men could have as many concubines as they desired was justified by the expectation of the continuation of the family line. The family values protected the family laws that treated women as inferior human beings.

Third, Ames and Hall state that the flexibility that permits a greater degree of creativity in the correlative model also permits a greater degree of abuse and grosser violations of human dignity (1998, 97). This is the only indication they give for why Chinese women's oppression seemed greater than that in the Western world. They suggest that there was some flexibility in such a correlative model, but that flexibility also could allow in degree "for a new configuration of the male/female roles" (99).

In reality, this suggestion is too optimistic; it could not be real if we look at women's actual lives under the social institutions of systematic sexism. Those institutions systematically fixed each gender's roles and made people believe in their fates as role players. If women did not fit into those subordinated roles and perfect them, they simply could not survive. If the man-made flexibility can lean in the opposite direction against women's inferiority, as Ames and Hall suggest, it must break up its social structure of male-domination. That definitely needs a combination of all efforts from various directions in pioneering works to deconstruct Confucianism, which is not what Ames and Hall expect to do.

In assessing the adequacy of an ethical theory, it is important to consider its implications for ethical practice. Feminist philosophers have shown that, in a deeply gendered social context, an ostensibly gender-neutral theory may have consequences that are disproportionately damaging for women. Neo-Confucianism's instructions for women definitely did more harm to women's status and increased women's oppression and subordination in their ethical practice. Unfortunately, this harm is not easy to clarify since it is hidden in a claim of mutual respect and reciprocity between men and women in the patriarchal society.

In order to turn the strongest social impacts of sexism in the opposite direction, we first need to dig out where those impacts came from and to expose the Confucian contributions to those sexist ideologies. I think the most damaging contribution of Confucians was their focus on the value of hierarchy, not on the value of difference. This is obvious in the Neo-Confucian literature. Although they point out the distinctive model of "correlative sexism," Ames and Hall do not differentiate between a value of hierarchy and a value of difference in a satisfactory way. It is the former that played a greater role in the practice of women's oppression.

My survey of the evolution of the Confucian view of women in Chinese history shows that most influential Confucians advocated women's inferior position and women's virtues of following the will of another. Only a few exceptions are scholars like Li Zhi (1527-1602) (see Lee's article, in Li Chenyang 2000). The cosmological argument of necessary hierarchy in a harmonious order was the ground for justifying those theories. The necessity of hierarchy and the value of hierarchy were continuously strengthened in Confucian theories and practices. Likewise, no serious challenges were raised nor investigations into the effects of those theories on women's everyday lives undertaken. Under Confucian instructions to women, women were to follow the will of another (father, husband, and son) and be untalented in order to avoid expressing their opinions. These virtues kept women away from independent thinking in their own lives and encouraged them to remain silent and submissive. In addition, so-called virtuous women made tremendous contributions to the continuation of a harmonious Chinese society. Respectable men and humble, oppressed women became the essence of the Confucian world.

An alternative way to see Confucianism will be: regardless of its view of women's oppression, Confucianism offers valuable thoughts on human nature and relational selfhood that are compatible with feminist investigations of ethical theory of the self. The Confucian concept of *ren* seems a precursor of an ethics of care, and a new version of care ethics should be connected with the feminist goal of ending women's oppression. Could we save Confucianism by deleting its view of women's inferiority and keeping its original thoughts of selfhood? This issue was raised in Ames and Hall's recent book, *The Democracy of the Dead* (1999). In my view, the issue of women's equality is inevitably related to issues of democracy that oppose a value of hierarchy. I will start to explore the relationship between these issues through the following chapters: women's formal equality in the May Fourth Movement, substantial equality in Mao's time, and equal opportunity in the post-Mao period. In the last chapter, I will develop a model of women's equality and democracy through the discussion of different viewpoints.

Notes

1. Wing-tsit Chan, *A Source Book in Chinese Philosophy* (Princeton, NJ: Princeton University Press, 1963), 271.
2. Roger T. Ames and David L. Hall, *The Democracy of the Dead: Dewey, Confucius, and the Hope for Democracy in China* (Chicago: Open Court, 1999).
3. There are two systems of romanization in Chinese: pinyin and Wade-Giles. The word *ren* is pinyin and the word *jen* is Wade-Giles, but the two refer to the same Chinese character. Other examples are: *song* (pinyin) and *sung* (Wade-Giles), *zhou* (pinyin) and *chou* (Wade-Giles), etc.
4. Yang Bo-jun, *Lunyu Yizhu (Interpretation of Analects)* (Beijing: Zhonghua Shuju, China Book Bureau, 1996), 18.
5. The English translations of *The Analects* are various. I use the most reliable interpretations: one is D. C. Lau (1979); the second is Arthur Waley (1938); the third is Wing-

tsit Chan (1963). I check them with the Chinese original and its interpretation by Yang Bo-jun (1996).

6. See "Chinese classics," in Routledge, *Concise Routledge Encyclopedia of Philosophy* (London: Routledge, 2000), 135-36. The five classics include *Zhouyi (Zhou Changes), Shangshu (Documents), Shijing (Odes), LiJi (The Book of Rites)*, and *ChunQiu FanLu (Spring and Autumn Annals)*.

7. These four scholars are universally recognized as experts in Chinese philosophy. I ignore the question of whether or not their interpretations of *The Analects* bear patriarchal characteristics and simply appropriate the valuable parts of their thoughts about Confucius.

8. Unless I am comparing different translations of the same passage, I will follow the practice of referencing the classical text using conventional section numbers rather than page numbers of the modern translations. See note 5 for information on the modern translations I have used.

9. In Chan's translation this section is in 6:28, but in original Chinese text it is in 6:30. See Yang Bo-jun's Chinese original and Lau's translation.

10. Here I follow most translations of Confucius's *jen* into "man," and I believe Confucius meant "man," but *jen* could be used in a gender-neutral way to refer to humans.

11. Confucius has a famous talk about this essence in *The Analects*. Tsai Yu asked about the three years' mourning and said he thought a year would be quite long enough. Confucius replied, "Would you then (after a year) feel at ease in eating good rice and wearing silk brocades? . . . If you would really feel at ease, then do so. But a true gentleman is in mourning, if he eats dainties, he does not relish them, if he hears music, it does not please him, if he sits in his ordinary seat, he is not comfortable. That is why he abstains from these things. But if you would really feel at ease, there is no need for you to abstain." When Tsai Yu had gone out, Confucius said, "How inhuman Yu is! Only when a child is three years old does it leave its parents arms. The three years' mourning is the universal mourning everywhere under Heaven. And Yu—was he not the darling of his father and mother for three years!" (7:21).

12. The book *Spring and Autumn Annals (ChunQiu FanLu)* is complicated and controversial but in general it represents Dong's basic philosophy and distinctive thought on the whole, therefore "it is nonproblematic to use it for a research" of Dong (Huang Pumin 1992, 71).

13. Mencius (Mengzi, fourth century B.C.) is best known for the book *Mengzi* and his idea of goodness in humans (see Routledge 2000, 563 and 135-36).

14. Both Confucius and his father gave up their wives according to *Family Jottings* (see Tang Ji-cang, "Women and Confucius," in *Selected Writings On Women's Issues During the May Fourth Period,* 1981, 161).

15. Cheng Yi (1033-1108) initiated a school called rationalistic scholarship that was completed by Zhu Xi (Cheng-Zhu Li Xue). Cheng Yi and his brother Cheng Hao (1032-1085) were known as the two Cheng masters (see Feng 1948, 281). Although Cheng and Zhu were not contemporaries, later Confucians called their work the Cheng-Zhu school because Zhu continued the tradition of the Neo-Confucianism of Cheng Yi and Cheng Hao.

16. Dai Zhen was famous for his focus on scholarship of *li*. He tried to combine the ideas of Mencius and Xunzi regarding goodness and evil in human nature (see Fang Litian 1990, 397-98).

17. Li is associate professor of philosophy and chair of the department of philosophy at Central Washington University. He was the first president (1995-1997) of the Association of Chinese Philosophers in America, the author of *The Tao Encounters The West* (1999), and the editor of *The Sage and the Second Sex: Confucius, Ethics, and Gender* (2000).

18. Tu is professor of Chinese history and philosophy and chairman of the Committee on the Study of Religion at Harvard University. He is the foremost exponent of Confucian thought in the United States today.

19. Margery Wolf, "Beyond the Patrilineal Self," in *Self as Person in Asian Theory and Practice,* ed. Roger Ames and David Hall (Albany: State University of New York Press, 1994), 254.

20. Ames is professor of philosophy and director of the Center for Chinese Studies at the University of Hawaii. He is the editor of *Philosophy East and West,* and *China Review International.* Among his recent works are *Thinking Through Confucius: Anticipating China; Thinking Through the Narrative of Chinese and Western Culture;* and *The Democracy of The Dead: Dewey, Confucius, and the Hope for Democracy in China,* all with David L. Hall (professor of philosophy at the University of Texas, El Paso).

Chapter Two

The May Fourth Era and Women's Formal Equality

The May Fourth Movement (1917-1919) stands as the Chinese Renaissance in the nation's history and has remained a significant topic among Chinese intellectuals as well as all of those people concerned with her progress in the pursuit of a good society. With the overthrow of the last imperial dynasty, the Manchu, in 1911 and the unstable new government of the Republic, China was in a turbulent situation with warlords competing for ruling power. Patriots and intellectuals brought in new social ideas and theories from the West in order to save China from the imperialist invasions on the one hand, and to criticize corrupt government and feudal ideologies on the other.

In this chapter I will briefly address the features and significance of the May Fourth spirit, emphasizing its feminist discourse. Then, I will focus on various views of women's issues: the thoughts of the Nationalist feminist thinker Qiu Jin and He Xiangning; a liberal feminist criticism of traditional ethics of women from Mao Zedong, Lu Xun, Hu Shi, and Wu Yu; Marxist feminism as articulated by Li Dazhao and Chen Duxiu; and, finally, views from the combined feminist thinkers: Xiang Jingyu and other women activists. I will argue that all forms of Chinese feminism during the May Fourth era (1915-1925) were limited to a common pursuit of formal equality, which was the ground for a united front against women's oppression. Because Chinese women were greatly oppressed in the past, it was difficult for them to pursue an independent movement for their equality and liberation, even though women's issues became a serious national issue during the May Fourth Movement when diversified ideologies clashed. This also elicits a question with regard to women's autonomy and a democratic pursuit of their equality. What is a democratic model for seeking women's equality? This question will appear throughout my whole project of examining models of sex equality and the exploration of its answer will continue through the following chapters.

General Features of the May Fourth Movement

After the Opium War (1839-1842), the first tide of the women's liberation movement in China emerged in a movement called Constitutional Reform[1] and Modernization. Reformers like Tan Zi-tong and Kang Yu-wei considered women's problems to be mainly a by-product of the feudal system, whereupon they advocated women's education and monogamy for both men and women, while opposing practices such as foot binding. All of these discussions and activities were, however, on a limited scale, and they receded even further after the Constitutional Reform movement failed. Subsequently, Britain and other imperialist invaders forced the Chinese government to allow their occupation of Hong Kong, Macao, and other small areas in cities within China. Leading Chinese intellectuals began to think about why the Constitutional Reform and other revolutionary activities had failed and, thus, how to carry out the task of overcoming imperialism and feudalism. They thought that the weakness of the nation originated from people's ignorance. Thus, they advocated a radical change in China's backward state, beginning with changing people's ethical beliefs. To do so, they believed, would reform people's souls with self-renewal and the power of will as Western philosopher Nietzsche advocated. These ideas of moral revolution and ethical enlightenment greatly influenced many patriots and intellectuals such as Mao Zedong, Li Dazhao, Lu Xun, Chen Duxiu, etc. During the May Fourth Movement, many serious writers addressed themselves to one or more substantive issues such as the reform of the family system, marriage and divorce, communal rearing of children, chastity, suicide, and suffrage.

In the book *From May Fourth to the New May Fourth* (Zhou 1989) many scholars on the New May Fourth[2] offer insightful reflections on both movements. Some of their comments and thoughts on May Fourth enhance our understanding of its great influence on China's history up to the present time. What was the central concern of the May Fourth Movement? Was it "how to rebuild Chinese culture" as Zhang Hao stated (1989, 66). Why did the Chinese need this rebuilding? China was proud of her three thousand years of brilliant culture prior to the Opium War,[3] but the turbulent situation—foreign invasions and the Chinese failure of resistance, conflicts between the Qing dynasty and local warlords, and the failure of the reform movements—made her cry for new ideas and practices to save the nation and the people. China was facing a test of her own cultural tradition and an urgent need for a new culture. Along with foreign military invasion came various Western ideologies that were imported into Chinese society and adopted by the intellectuals during the late nineteenth and early twentieth centuries.

Hu Shi[4] described the May Fourth Movement as the Chinese Renaissance and distinguished it from other historical movements: Its leaders knew their mission. "They want to instill into the people a new outlook on life which shall free them from the shackles of tradition and make them feel at home in the new world and its new civilization" (Hu 1963, 44). Hu also emphasized that this new civilization could not be born without an intimate contact with Western culture: "Contact with strange civilizations brings new standards of value with which the native culture is re-examined and re-evaluated, and conscious reformation and regeneration are the natural outcome of such trans-valuation of values. Without the benefit of an intimate contact with the civilization of the West, there could not be the Chinese Renaissance." For instance, for ten long centuries the bound feet of Chinese women were regarded as beautiful by a peculiar perversion of aesthetic appreciation under the influence of Neo-Confucian ethics, "but it took only a few decades of contact with foreign peoples and ideas to make the Chinese people see the ugliness and inhumanity of this institution" (44-47).

What were the predominant features of the May Fourth Movement in calling for a new civilization? First, the motivation of the movement was anti-imperialism, saving China from foreign domination. Obviously, Chinese short knives and long spears could not protect the country from foreign guns and modern steamships. "Science" and "Democracy" immediately became the two big terms as slogans for the movement since these two were considered to be "the key to rebuild Chinese culture" (Zhou 1989, 70).

However, how did the May Fourth scholars as new culturalists understand "Democracy" in a Chinese context? Their concept of democracy is best understood as articulated by Chen Duxiu,[5] a new leader of the intellectual class, who fought against Confucian doctrines as a basic system of moral education in China. Chen showed how Confucianism had justified and rationalized the political institution of despotic rule in China, and he believed that Confucianism must disappear along with unlimited monarchy. He points out: "The morals taught by Confucius and his school belonged to the age of feudalism and are mostly unsuited to an age of democracy" (Hu 1963, 90). The spirit of democracy was expressed by rebelling against all traditions, radically criticizing old thoughts, and by seeking freedom and equality, especially women's equality.

Why did women's issues such as oppression, equality, rights, and education become the significant theme in the May Fourth Movement? The new culturists found that Western ideologies—social Darwinism, liberalism, anarchism, socialism, Marxism, and feminism—provided them with a position outside of the dominant Confucian ideology that enabled them to claim themselves the creators of a new culture. Adopting a humanist position from Western liberalism, the new culturalists concentrated their critique on the "inhumanness" of Confucianism. The three cardinal principles of Confucianism were held responsible for making the Chinese slaves: The ruler guides the subject; the father guides the son; and the husband guides the wife. If the Chinese ever wanted to establish a modern democratic republic, the new culturists argued, they must replace Confucian principles with freedom, equality, and independence. These modern, liberal values were thus used as liberating tools to free the people's benighted minds. Rebelling against the traditional values, attacking Confucianism, and advocating a Western liberal concept of human rights at that historical juncture necessarily led to an inclusion of women. As Wang Zheng stated, "a wholesale offensive against Confucianism had to include an attack on gender hierarchy. More important to the New Culturalists, the social institutions based on this principle provided ample evidence of the inhumanness of Confucianism" (1999, 12).

Many journals were devoted to the subject of women, but the writers and the audience were predominantly male because more than 90 percent of the female population was illiterate. As Li Xiaojiang points out, male intellectuals were "the first to raise women's issues" (1994, 138). These scholars viewed the feminist suffrage movement as necessary and as a sign of modernity in the developing Chinese society. If China was to become modern and democratic, Chinese women had to be emancipated and achieve equal status as human beings. The link between the status of women and the nation's status in the modern world made the themes of women's emancipation, human rights, and modernization integral to the New Culture movement. Later these liberalist scholars divided into two rival parties: the nationalist and the Communist.

The 1911 Revolution toppled the Qing (the Manchu), the last of China's dynasties, and strove to replace it with a republic and a constitutional regime. In the following decade, China was fragmented and dominated by militarists, this warlord period lasting until 1928, when the Guomindang (GMD) National Revolutionary Army unified most of China. However, the Chinese Communist Party (CCP) and Red Army occupied some areas in Jiangxi province. The CCP was established in 1921, while the GMD was reorganized in accordance with the Soviet model in 1923-1924.[6] Hence, the stage was set for a decades-long rivalry between the two Leninist parties, which culminated with the CCP victory in 1949.

The Nationalist Party (GMD) was founded in 1911 by Sun Zhongshan (Sun Yatsen; 1866-1925) and his colleagues in the Revolutionary Alliance. Organized in Japan in 1905, the party had goals of overthrowing the Qing and establishing a republican government in China. Sun was elected president and later became a powerful symbolic leader of the Chinese revolution. Sun advocated "Three Principles of the People" to summarize his political and social concepts. These principles represented Chinese nationalism, democracy, and people's livelihood or social welfare. Under these principles the GMD and the CCP cooperated until 1927, when Chiang Kai-shek (1887-1975) launched the White Terror to execute Communists. People called him a traitor to Sun's three New Policies under the three Principles: an alliance with the U.S.S.R, support for workers' and peasants' movements, and collaboration with the CCP (Perkins 1999, 492-95).

The Chinese Communist Party (CCP) was born in 1921, and many of her founders, including Li Dazhao and Chen Duxiu, were famous scholars of the May Fourth spirit. Though they kept their distance from so-called "bourgeois feminism," these male communists supported feminist ideas for ending women's oppression. With the help of the funds and programs of the CCP and the GMD, female communists such as Xiang Jingyu, Wang Huiwu, Deng Yingchao, and other feminist activists in the GMD did pioneering work for the women's movements against women's oppression. They were, however, discouraged from leading an independent women's movement. Issues about feminism, nationalism, and communism were raised in the revolutionary period of the 1920s. From the first decade of the twentieth century to the May Fourth Movement of 1919 to the May Thirtieth Incident of 1925 to the GMD's purge of communists in 1927, we will see ups and downs in the women's movement's fight against oppression.

Nationalist Feminist Thought Before the May Fourth Era

Feminism emerged in China together with the rise of nationalism in the first decade of the twentieth century. Many publications called for Chinese men and women to rise up against the Manchu dictatorship, the last generation of the Qing dynasty. Radical revolutionaries regarded the corrupted Qing as the obstacle to women's liberation. Thus, obtaining women's rights became inseparable from an anti-Manchu position, and participation in the anti-Qing government meant the beginning of an actual process of achieving women's rights (Wang Zheng 1999, 42).

Among nationalist feminists, Qiu Jin (Chiu Chin; 1875-1907) was the pioneer fighter in the women's movement. She was beheaded at the age of 31 in 1907, when she was caught leading an abortive anti-dynastic uprising. However, Qiu Jin came to be considered a martyr to Chinese nationalism and a model for rebellion against the enemies of China. Qiu had two major goals in her life: to overthrow the despotic Qing government in a revolutionary uprising, and to strive for women's equality, education, and independence (Luo 1996, 470-71). Qiu was full of enthusiasm for organizing political activities to achieve nationalist goals in Sun Zhongshan's Revolutionary Alliance in Japan. In her poem, "Women's Right," Qiu expressed her wishes for women: "We want our emancipation! For our liberty we'll drink a cup. Men and Women are born equal. Why should we let men hold sway? We will rise and save ourselves. Ridding the nation of all her shame. In the steps of Joan of Arc, with our own hands will we regain our land" (Bingham and Gross 1980, 34).

In another poem, Qiu expressed her spirit of "Dare to Die" as a martyr to Chinese nationalism. The American reporter Helen Snow made a comment that "her tomb in Hangzhou was the only woman's tomb in China to which the Chinese made pilgrimages" (Bingham and Gross 1980, 34).

Qiu had a strong nationalist concern for China's future. The Western invasion of China convinced her that China was on the brink of disaster, and all Chinese should work for the country's salvation. She believed that China was on the verge of extinction in a struggle against the more vigorous imperialist West, that nationalism could save China through revolution to overthrow the rotten Qing dynasty and to wake the country to gain the strength for survival. She argued that equal education and rights would kindle women's patriotic desire to contribute to national strength and would elicit contributions toward the new civilization that might be less tainted with traditional aspirations than were those of men (Wolf 1975, 48-49).

Qiu also wrote many articles advocating women's rights in the *Chinese Women's Journal,* which she founded. She firmly believed that to achieve equal rights, women had to take on the responsibilities of citizenship. She wrote: "Equality between men and women is endowed by Heaven. How can we be content to lag behind? Our fair hands are needed in order to recover our rivers and mountains. Taking responsibility on our shoulders we citizen heroines must never fail to live up to our expectations" (Wang 1999, 43).

By 1907, there were a number of women in the revolutionary parties, but most were there to perform secondary roles such as managing party fronts, distributing radical literature, and setting up temporary cells. Qiu was the only one to lead a major attempt to overthrow the government. She shared with many other radical intellectuals of her day a naïve faith that overthrowing the dynasty would purge the country of corrupt and weakening influences, ushering in a new era of national strength and individual freedom. However, she never clearly defined all these aims and relations during her short but very devoted life to political activities. It was obvious Qiu placed revolution ahead of feminist goals, and this anticipated both post-May Fourth leftist women and later gender equality achieved in the People's Republic. Unlike the Communists and other socialists, Qiu did not advocate union with the masses, though her writings suggest real sympathy for the common people. Qiu saw that radical revolution was necessary for women's eventual liberation and implicitly recognized that sexual equality was not likely to be achieved without some major structural changes. Therefore, she was honored as an outstanding example of developing women's achievements in the national cause rather than in the primary feminist cause.

Influenced by Qiu's model, many women joined the revolutionary parties and military drills to play roles in revolutionary events, operations, and organization. After the Qing was toppled and the Republic government established, many women began a militant women's suffrage movement. Tang Qunying, a classmate of Qiu, and an early member of the Revolutionary Alliance, became the most prominent leader. Tang and others formed various women's organizations to pursue women's equality in the new Republic. She led a group of suffragists to petition the national council in March 1912, but they were denied access to the council. They felt outraged by this betrayal and the fact that their militancy had not helped them win suffrage in 1912. This betrayal clearly showed that women could not only shoulder their duties as citizens, but also fight for the rights of citizenship (Wang 1999, 129-30). This fight became significant at the national level during the May Fourth era.

He Xiangning (1878-1972) was also a feminist anti-Manchu revolutionary. She joined Sun Zhongshan's Revolutionary Alliance in Tokyo in 1905 and later persuaded her husband, Liao Zhongkai, to be a member of the party as well. Liao became the second-most powerful leader in Sun's revolutionary organization but was assassinated by the right wing of the GMD in 1925. He Xiangning continued to be an active leader of the Central Women's Department until the United Front, along with the CCP, collapsed in mid-1927.

He Xiangning had long-standing interests in women's rights issues. As a child in a middle-class business family, she refused to have her feet bound. She joined the Revolutionary Alliance without consulting her husband. During her position as the director of the Central Women's Department, she stressed the importance of promoting women's issues in the context of the wider struggle to win the nationalist revolution. She chose to focus her attention on developing programs that would promote women's practical interests in the new order, such as drafting legal codes to protect women, developing a cadre school, urging the government to hire women, and organizing a women's Red Cross unit, etc. (Gilmartin 1995, 161-62). She stressed the great importance of women becoming involved in the revolutionary effort for nationalist reasons, and in the 1920s she did impressive work in leading and supporting the women's movement in the United Front of the two parties, the GMD and the CCP.

The connection between nationalism and feminism during the first two decades of the twentieth century became more firmly planted in Chinese soil. The essential bond between these two movements did not rule out concern for the "women question." The oppression of women was portrayed as one more example of the inhumanity of Confucian culture and society. Thus, the solution to women's problems was exactly the same as the solution to the general national crisis.

Liberal Feminist Thought During the May Fourth Movement

In this section I will examine different views of women in liberal feminist thinking during the May Fourth Movement: first, Mao's early view of women, emphasizing women's equal rights; second, Lu's radical criticism of inhumanity in the Confucian view of women and Hu's modest critique of the traditional view of women's chastity; and, last, Wu Yu's criticism of the Confucian view of filial piety. All of these liberal critics were men.

Mao studied both classical Confucianism and the Western thought of Kant, Mill, Nietzsche, Paulsen, etc., and he kept his critical eye on both cultural heritages. During the May Fourth period, Mao's thought had been changing and gradually shifted to Western Marxism; yet Mao's ideas and views of women expressed the influences of liberalism, seeking democracy and the freedom of individuals, the spirit of self-realization and abstract humanity. He wrote many articles calling upon young people to make their own decisions about marriage, organizing women to arm against their oppression, and to be independent and realize their own will and ideas. All of these articles were published in journals such as *New Youth, New People Study Society, Hsiang River Review, Women's Bell*, and *TaKung Bao*, and were collected into one book in 1990: *Early Writings of Mao Zedong 1912.6-1920.11*, which stands as the only representation of Mao's early view of women. Mao said on behalf of women: "As we are all human beings, why not grant us all suffrage? And as we are all human beings, why not allow us to mix freely with one another?" (Mao 1990, 375).

In the following, Mao attacked the use of chastity as a measuring-stick for morality: "What sort of chastity is this, completely confined to women with shrines for female martyrs everywhere? Where are the shrines for chaste boys?" (Mao 1990, 375).

Mao showed great sympathy and support for suffering women, and he cried out in their voice: "Misery! Misery! Where is the god of freedom? Help us immediately! We are wakening now, we must be united with all sisters! Sweep away the goblins that destroy physical and spiritual freedom" (Mao 1990, 375-76).

All of these criticisms represent Mao's strong opposition to feudal morality, his aspirations for individual freedom and happiness, and his great concern for women's situation. While criticizing and revealing the evils of the old morality, Mao encouraged women to unite and participate in a revolutionary movement to break out of the prisons made by men's authority. According to Mao's viewpoint, women needed to be armed with weapons instead of with rouge and face powder. This was a very brave and new idea that considered women the same as men and opposed the old popular customs of treating women as playmates, pets, or slaves of men. In his *Great Union of Popular Masses,* Mao also pointed out sharply that valuing the so-called "virtuous wife and mother" was not for women's good, but for training each woman "to be a permanent prostitute for her husband" (1990, 375), and for keeping them within feudal bounds to serve one man uniquely. This is a very radical critique to reveal that the substance of feudal rituals is to deceive and oppress women.

Through his investigation of the reasons for women's oppression, Mao argued that though women's reproductive functions hindered them, the real source of their oppression was the immorality of men. Mao questioned why women had been oppressed by men for thousands of years. It was not that women were deficient when compared with men; instead, Mao thought, men and women were not very different from each other either in their psychology or physiology in general. The only difference was women's biological function—procreation. According to Mao, during pregnancy, women were unable to perform hard physical labor and needed the help of men; men took advantage of women's vulnerable situation and supported them with food at the price of their subordination.

Mao was also concerned with women's rights to education, because he thought education was vital to women in preparation for their economic independence. He criticized the unfair allotment of educational funds for women. The whole nation's educational fund in 1920 amounted to 2,150,000 yuan, but women's schools were given less than 100,000 yuan. Mao said ironically: "One part was compared with the other twenty-one (in the above amounts), men, how cruel you are to treat women this way" (1990, 547). Realizing the serious problem of women's education, Mao encouraged a women's leader, Xiang Jingyu, to bring more sisters to study abroad. He believed that women could get better education abroad and that education had a vital role in women becoming self-supporting.

Mao's early theory concerning women's rights to education, individual freedom, and the moral reasons for women's oppression reflects his support for liberal thought. He also emphasized economic independence, which, among other concerns, led to his conversion to Marxism in 1921.

Lu Xun's[7] 1918 article, "My Views on Chastity," presents a sharp critique of the Confucian view of chastity. He raises three questions regarding chastity, which clearly expose and discredit the single-sided view of women's chastity. The first question is: Is chastity a moral virtue? Lu argues that if something can count as moral, it should be applied to all people and be beneficial to all. "Virtue should be universal, required of all . . . as well as oneself." Why are only women required to be chaste by Confucian moralists? And "all men are excluded from what goes by the name of chastity today, not even all women are eligible for this honor."[8]

Lu interprets the Confucian view of what women should do in the case of rape: when women are attacked, they must commit suicide before being defiled, otherwise, they will not be deserving of the honor of the glorious martyr. Old morals neither blamed the man on whom she depended of cowardice and incompetence in protecting her, nor were they concerned with how to punish the criminal. But the victim would be condemned universally if she lost her chastity. She had only one choice to keep her honor: she had to die as quickly as she could. This "is absolutely inhuman" (ACWF 1981, 118).

The second question Lu raises is about who has the authority to judge women's chastity. As he points out, the authority to appraise women's chastity is always male. Do they have any authority to ask women to be chaste while they enjoy polygamy (concubinage)? The old moralists would say that men are different from women, and this difference comes from the ancient concept of yang and yin. Lu argues that there is no way of proving that yang, or man, is nobler than yin, or woman. We must accept the truth that the two sexes should be equally regarded. If equal, they should be bound by the same contract. "Men cannot make rules for women which they do not keep themselves" (ACWF 1981, 118).

The final question Lu posits regards the cause of women's unchastity. He argues: according to the Confucian moralists' view, chastity only matters with one sex—female, and they never explore the cause of female unchastity. We all know that a woman could lose her chastity only through a man as offender. The old moralists blamed the woman alone while the man who destroyed her reputation went free from moral trial. Is this not the logic of male hegemony? According to this absurd logic, women must remain chaste while men can be polygamous. Such logic creates a perverted morality for submission: it is the cardinal wifely virtue. As Lu criticizes, women's chastity is absolutely meaningless because it justifies persecution of women (ACWF 1981, 119).

Lu's criticism addresses the heart of the traditional Confucian value of chastity by exposing its inhumanity and the male hegemony which created and nourished it. Women's bound feet and the custom of keeping concubines were so popular and compatible with the traditional ideology that most Chinese were apathetic to their evils. Lu's article played a leading role in the critique of the Confucian view of women.

Hu Shi (1891-1962), a Ph.D. who returned to China from the United States and was also deeply influenced by Confucianism, expresses his disagreement with the Confucian view of chastity. In regard to the issue of women's chastity, Hu analyzes the unequal attitudes and treatment of different sexes in Confucianism. He argues: if chastity is important and necessary for women to be virtuous, it must be the same for men to be virtuous. But, in fact, polygamous men retain their reputations in society while remarried women have no public credibility. Hu claims he does not advocate any free affairs outside marriage, but men and women should be valued by the same moral standard (Hu 1986 [1918], 49-50). Hu explains that chastity is concerned with the relationship between a couple. A wife should respect her husband's love, and the husband should respect hers; otherwise, he will not deserve respect and chastity. "This is exactly what Confucius said: Do not impose on others what you yourself do not desire" (50). He holds a view that Confucius himself should not advocate single-sex ethics, although Confucius does not discuss the issue of women's chastity.

Obviously, Hu uses Confucius's own words to attack the later Confucian view of women's chastity. As I argued in chapter 1, the Neo-Confucian view of women after Song (960 A.D.) played a leading role in guiding the secular ethics of women. Hence, the Neo-Confucian view of women's chastity or the secular ethics of women's inferiority should be the causes indicating how women suffered from the old customs that devalued women. Hu does not give a detailed analysis about whether the later Confucians distort their master's thought or not, but he clearly separates them and criticizes the latter as violating Confucius's golden rule.

Nevertheless, the Confucian concept of *ren* does not equally apply to women's ethical experiences as it applies to men's situations. Because of the gender hierarchy, the golden rule was not equally applicable to women as it was to men. This topic needs much more attention and a deep exploration of it could not develop in the context of the rebellious spirit during the May Fourth Movement.

The fourth liberal critic of Confucian ethics is Wu Yu. He reveals how the concept of filial piety affects women's lives. According to the *Book of Rites*, one of the classics of Confucian texts, there are many kinds of non-piety, but the worst one is sterility. To be filially pious, one must have sons who can continue the family line. According to Confucius, the difference between women and men is determined at the moment they are born: a boy was more valuable than a girl since he could carry on the family fortune. A girl infant was in danger of being drowned if the family did not want her as a potential financial loss (rearing her until her marriage to another family). A woman who had no sons would be in the worst situation: she would either be put aside or sent back to her father. Sterility was used to support the system of concubines or polygamy, and women were primarily tools used to continue the male family line. Wu points out that the assumption that sterility is the worst in filial piety is extremely absurd and immoral. It leads people to be slaves to their ancestry rather than equally respected with equal concerns and responsibilities. He suggests that we should be persons who care for and help each other with respect and humility.[9]

The issue of filial piety is the core of Confucian ethical discussions. The critic represents the rebellion against the traditional ethical popularity rather than a careful examination of this concept. However, the criticism reveals the absurdity of the belief that women and men are different by birth because of its pro-single-sex view: the importance and value of the male as the person to carry on the family line.

All of the above liberal feminist critiques of the pro-male sex morality in Confucianism exposed the unequal treatment of women in Confucian ethics and caused women to seek a modern value of freedom and equality for all individuals.

Marxist Feminist Thought in the May Fourth Movement

The women's suffrage movement in the United States during the first two decades of the twentieth century, with its ideas of gender equality in politics, deeply influenced Chinese society. Inspired by feminist ideas of women's equality, Chinese Marxists raised various criticisms of the traditional view of women. It led them to ponder how Chinese women could be liberated from their oppressed situations. I will discuss three Marxist criticisms against women's oppression, presented by two men, Li Dazhao and Chen Duxiu, and one woman, Xiang Jin-gyu.

Li Dazhao[10] claimed in 1922: "The twentieth century is the era of liberating the oppressed classes, a time of women's emancipation, too. It is the time that women are seeking their self and men are discovering women's significance."[11] Li argues that real democracy must include women's liberation. Chinese society never allowed women to be involved in public life, and it set strict boundaries between men and women, leading to a dictatorial system of male hegemony. Not only did men dominate women, but also, some men dominated other men. "Real democracy with a state of women's liberation is what we need to change our society."[12] Li also makes an important point that the situation of all women is not the same, because they belong to different classes: "The interests of middle-class women cannot be said as all women's interests; the claims they made for their rights cannot represent all women's liberation." Therefore, there are two fundamentally different issues here: on the one hand, all women need to unite to fight against the dictatorial system of men's society; on the other hand, all prole-tarian class women need to unite their class, both men and women, to overthrow the exploiting social system.[13]

In this short speech, we see that Li does not develop his view of the two kinds of oppressions and how the two relate to each other and whether in prac-tice they conflict with each other or not. However, he does indicate that women are divided by different interests and needs. The Western suffrage movement focuses mainly on middle-class women's interests, and it may not include the interests of working women completely. Li's view has great significance for later development of the women's liberation movement in China. Mao's later view of women is also influenced by the same considerations. As the founder of the CCP, Li's view certainly expresses Engels's orthodoxy in explaining women's oppression. Engels argues, in *The Origin of The Family, Private Prop-erty, and the State*, that private ownership and class exploitation were the origins of women's oppression. Therefore, the only way to get women's liberation was to end class exploitation.

The second critique, made by Chen Duxiu, emphasizes social change and socialism, which is compatible with Li's suggestion for social changes. Chen argues that if we see women's issues such as education, public jobs, communi-cation, and so on, as piecemeal, there is no systematic way to solve these prob-lems. Women's suffering could be traced back to their loss of personality. They had no independent personhood according to the traditional ethical canon. The Threefold Obedience rules made them subordinate to all men, and they led mis-erable lives. Nevertheless, the root of women's suffering always relates to eco-nomic reasons. In Chen's analysis, women's economic independence is crucial to ending their oppression. In a word, women's issues ultimately relate to eco-nomic independence. But women's economic independence can only become true under the socialist system. To Chen, socialism means to assist the weak against the stronger. Women are the weak as labor workers; hence, women's issues can only be solved under socialism, and a socialist society is the only one in which women's liberation becomes reality. The radical and complete solution of women's suffering is to strive for a socialism that advocates the unity of the poor and the weak against the rich and the powerful. Only socialism can wipe out the root of all oppressions including women's oppression.[14]

Chen's view of women's emancipation expresses the Marxist view of women's issues, which became the dominant view in the later women's movement under the lead of the Chinese Communist Party. Chinese women's situation under the feudal social system was different from the proletarian working class women's situation in the Western countries. The method of liberating Chinese women would not be the same as that in which other women changed their positions. Chen points out that women's liberation must be part of the liberation of all the oppressed, although he does not give a specific analysis of how Chinese women could gain liberation. Chen is correct to put women's issues under the test of a social system. Socialism always tries to make an egalitarian society by using social protection programs for disadvantaged people, such as women and minorities. Women might be economically independent with the help of socialist programs and policies. In my view, however, gender oppression is not merely a matter of economic oppression. It will require the resolution of many complicated issues before women are finally emancipated. Chen does not give a convincing analysis about how women could be liberated when the exploiting class is abolished, so his view seems too brief and superficial.

The third critique, by Xiang Jingyu, explores a precondition of women's liberation, the abolition of private ownership. She argues that, as long as the old family system remains, women have no way to attain liberation. Only at a time that individual basic living needs—food, shelter, clothing, etc.—become socially provided will women achieve emancipation. Before that day we should work out concrete plans to push social changes step by step.[15]

It must be emphasized that the idea of breaking the traditional family system sounds very radical and explosive to Chinese people. Xiang was a leading Communist feminist in the public world of the 1920s. Although her view of women's liberation agrees in some respects with Li and Chen's Marxist view of women, she sees the problem of the private family more clearly. In Xiang's analysis, both the traditional Chinese family and the Western-type family are based on individual hedonism in abstraction and on private ownership; yet, private interests cannot be compatible with the goal of all people's happiness in the society. Hence, as long as the private family system survives, there is no hope for liberating women. Only when all our basic necessities, such as rearing children, nursing the old, health care, etc., become the society's responsibilities and the society organizes all people to coordinate for solving all these needs, can women realize true liberation. This final goal seems far in the future and highly idealistic. But Xiang does give a concrete plan to push society forward toward the destination. She gives several suggestions as concrete steps.

First, women must organize and unite to do research collectively on women's issues. At the time only a few women consciously recognized women's issues. We should have special organizations, permanent publishing journals, and enthusiastic participants. Also, we should unite with males who are aware of women's issues to discuss life issues together. We need to make strenuous efforts for our great cause.

Second, an alliance for self-determining marriage is urgently needed, since freedom of marriage is almost impossible under the old social pressure for arranged marriage by parents. Individual resistance against the evil of old customs, as sadly carried out by Ms. Zhao in Hunan, Li in Guangxi, and others, was a painful lesson. (All of them committed suicide to protest against arranged marriage.) Women could help by immediately organizing massive alliances to save other potential victims.

Third, educational opportunity is a foundation for personal development. Men and women should have equal opportunity and accessibility to education. But educational opportunities disproportionately favor male students above female students. This is not only unfortunate for women, but also presents a loss for society. According to Xiang, women's organizations must establish foundations in banks to provide for women's education and also encourage other forms of organizations to help.

The three critics, Li, Chen, and Xiang, share features of contemporary Western feminist thought. All would fight against women's subordination and seek the equality of men and women in the political arena, legal rights, freedom of marriage and divorce, educational opportunity, employment, etc. Xiang goes much further than the other male thinkers in criticizing the family system and calling for something like women's empowerment. Their critical thinking on women's oppression played an extremely important role in waking the whole nation to reevaluate the traditional authority of Confucianism regarding women's issues, especially Confucianism's insistence on women's chastity and obedience. By exposing the evilness and inhumanity of forcing women to be chaste at a price of suicide, May Fourth critics educated the public to realize the political alliance between traditional ethics and women's oppression. Their radical critiques make it clear that male hegemony and man-made family law are at the root of women's oppression. The radical exposure of these issues was made possible under the guise of democratic discussion in the turbulent period of the century's first and second decades. No absolute autocratic government was able to dominate Chinese society until the GMD unified China in 1928. Obviously, feminism could grow and flourish only in diversity and democracy.

Women's Mobilization and the United Front of the Women's Movement

In the above sections, I have discussed several different theoretical views of women's chastity, women's liberation, and formal equality. In this section, I will focus on several women leaders, emphasizing how they accomplished feminist goals in the CCP policy on women's issues and how their actions differed from those of the male feminists in the party. Although male feminist thinkers supported the idea of women's equality, they were not completely immune to the traditional pattern of male-dominant thinking. The CCP and the left-wing GMD supported the women's movements against the old ideologies with funding, media support, and decision-making in policies, but they would not allow any independent women's movements for women's special interests in issues of marriage, family relations, etc. Female communist feminists such as Wang Huiwu, Xiang Jingyu, Deng Yingchao, and Cai Chang, as the highest female representatives in the party, played pioneering roles in forging close links between feminism and communism, as well as in allying with nationalist feminists and unifying other women's groups in the United Front to fight for women's emancipation during the 1920s.

Wang Huiwu: The First Leader in a Women's Program of the CCP

Wang was the spouse of Li Da, one of the highest-ranking male leaders in the party, but she had her own reputation as the author of a prominent essay, "The Chinese Women Question: Liberation from a Trap," published in the autumn of 1919 in *Young China*. In this essay, Wang bitterly assailed the arranged-marriage system as a form of lifelong imprisonment for women. She argued that as soon as women accepted their womanhood as advocated by certain traditional norms, they were blinded to the real nature of their subjugation. Later on, a male communist feminist, Mao Dun,[16] strongly rebuked Wang's view in that essay. He wrote that although he was a defender of the cause of women's emancipation, he was deeply concerned that Wang's essay would encourage women to see men as inherently evil enemies. However, despite Mao Dun's objection to Wang's view, other male members still appreciated her efforts in helping the party's first congress. After a police officers' raid, she secured two sites for the meetings and reorganized the reconvening of the congress on a houseboat on West Lake in Zhejiang (her hometown). Her role at the congress paved the way for her acceptance as the leader of the women's program: she was empowered to revitalize the Shanghai Federation of Women's Circles (see Gilmartin 1995, 49-52). Despite her important role in the party's first congress and her appointment as leader of the women's program, Wang's formal membership remained a problem only to be discovered later. She was assumed to be a member because of being the wife of Li Da, who was one of the founders of the CCP.

In reorganizing the Shanghai Federation, Wang worked with another woman leader, Gao Junmin (the spouse of Chen Duxiu), on two projects: a women's journal entitled *Women's Voice* and a school for girls named Shanghai Pingmin Girl's School. Both projects ran well for one school year until Wang stepped down. *Women's Voice* was, significantly, the first party-sponsored journal that really presented female voices. The main message conveyed in the journal was that conscious women needed to broaden their political orientation and become leaders for the cause of working class women. The journal also strove to convey an international perspective by reporting on women's organizations in the Soviet Union and extolling the virtues of the female revolutionary martyr Rosa Luxemburg (Gilmartin 1995, 57). The journal became a useful forum for women to express their ideas in writing.

The difference between male and female perspectives was clearly shown in the debate over the issue of birth control. Both Wang Huiwu and Wang Jianhong wrote essays to express strong support for birth control as advocated by Margaret Sanger, who came to China in 1922 (Gilmartin 1995, 57). Wang Jianhong stressed that the adoption of birth control measures would enable women to reclaim their humanity. Wang Huiwu echoed the theme of economic independence and stressed that birth control would improve the quality of life for the entire human race, as well as give much greater freedom to women. She also believed that the practice of birth control actually served to enhance rather than detract from women's maternal instincts by reducing the physiological and psychological pain associated with many births, thereby allowing women to enjoy nurturing one or two children.

In opposition to Wang's support of reproductive rights for women, male author Mao Dun presented the standard Communist critique of birth control. According to this view, it was not excessive population but rather the unequal distribution of wealth and services that was the reason for poverty. In Mao's view, the issue of birth control diverted women from engaging in the struggle to bring about fundamental social and economic change. This opinion dominated the debate over population growth after the establishment of the People's Republic of China in 1949, until the party adopted its one-child family policy in the late 1970s. Unfortunately, both Wangs' female perspectives on birth control were totally ignored or rebuked by the party.

The two projects of *Women's Voice* and the Pingmin Girl's School were shut down in the fall of 1922. It was said that there were several reasons behind the unraveling of this first women's program. Ding Ling[17] suggested that the Communist male leadership was unhappy with some of the content of the articles in *Women's Voice*: the leaders of the party perceived the journal as manifesting certain anarchist tendencies. And most importantly, Wang Huiwu's power in the party seriously eroded because her husband Li was not reelected to the Central Committee of the CCP. Finally, another couple took over this couple's positions through party decision. Cai Hesen (an ardent Marxist and a close friend of Mao Zedong) replaced Li Da, and his wife Xiang Jingyu took on the task of the women's movement, shortly after their return from France in late 1921. Xiang had the same formal membership problem as Wang.

Xing Jingyu: The First Director of the Women's Department of the CCP

One of the most difficult issues for Xiang when she was appointed Director of the Chinese Communist Women's Bureau in the summer of 1922 was to define the direction of this program. She was familiar with the animosity between feminists and socialists in France, and she tried to keep her distance from the bourgeois feminists in the Western world. At the beginning of her program, she distanced herself from the founding of a Women's Rights League and for a short time from other endeavors of women's work. Nevertheless, she had a special concern about the relationship of her program with unconnected independent women's organizations that had mushroomed throughout Chinese urban centers in the wake of the May Fourth protests. The newly established Women's Bureau seemed eminently reasonable from the standpoint of her May Fourth political and personal experiences, but posed a serious dilemma for this recent convert to Communism. Is feminism incompatible with Marxism within a particular Chinese context? Xiang struggled to come to terms with the theoretical and practical incompatibilities between gender and class. "In doing so, she had to take into consideration the mixed views of her comrades, the impact of the formation of an alliance between the nationalist and the communist parties (the United Front), the practical realities of women's organizing at that time, and the sentiments of her husband and close comrade, Cai Hesen" (Gilmartin 1995, 72). Indeed, Xiang made distinctive contributions to promoting a radical alteration of gender relations in the revolutionary movement, as well as for combating gender oppression within the party in the 1920s.

Xiang argued that women could not be genuinely emancipated until collective institutions, such as public nurseries, replaced the family. Obviously, her Communist orientation to women's issues reflected some indication of the continuation of her May Fourth feminist ideals, particularly her proposal that women should establish associations to promote free-choice marriage and thereby facilitate the termination of the arranged-marriage system. Her consistent attempts at combining nationalism, feminism, and communism shaped her enormous endeavors to organize a "general women's movement," an association of all women's groups in the United Front (Gilmartin 1995, 84).

Xiang was not alone in seeking to reconcile the national, feminist, and communist ideals; the CCP third congress clearly had made this one of its goals, and the eminent leader Li Dazhao strongly supported the women's rights movement. The party was seeking an alliance with Sun's Nationalist Party (Gilmartin 1995, 85). Xiang supported the party's policy of collaborating with the Nationalist Party and wholeheartedly endorsed the United Front through her position in the Communist Women's Bureau. Indeed, she made a significant contribution to constructing various women's programs in the Nationalist Party.

In the politics of collaboration, the first thing Xiang chose to implement was collaboration on women's groups and issues by gaining approval from the Nationalist Party leader to edit a new journal, entitled *Women's Weekly*. From 1923 to 1926, *Women's Weekly* carried articles on a wide range of topics such as love, sexuality, morality, and consciousness. Xiang contributed more than thirty articles to *Women's Weekly* to promote "the human rights and civil rights of women" (Gilmartin 1995, 88).

To Xiang, the only way to develop a truly "mass" women's movement was to integrate the struggle of feminist groups with those of the workers, and the "miserable state" of women workers should get the attention of women's right advocates. She made efforts to keep in touch with at least a dozen other women's groups in Shanghai. She proposed constructing an organizational foundation among various sectors of women in the heart of the National Party, and it won approval in the Communist congress. Forty members including Xiang and other women Communists joined the National Party in order to promote the national movement. In April of 1924, Xiang was named as the head of the Shanghai Women's Movement Committee of the National Party. This committee was to accomplish four tasks: (1) develop contact with women professionals, workers, students, and housewives; (2) stress the importance of disseminating education to the common people; (3) unify all women's groups; and (4) publicize other socialist countries' practices concerning women (Gilmartin 1995, 93). Through these devotions to the committee and in running *Women's Weekly,* Xiang laid the organizational foundation for mass mobilization of women in the National Revolution. The All-Women's Association created by Xiang was transformed into a women's mass mobilization organization that was established under a variety of names (different women's groups) in both urban and rural areas throughout much of China.

In 1926, the CCP sent Xiang to Moscow for political study, which meant that her status in the party changed because her marriage to Cai Hesen began to flounder. The Nationalist Party decided to suspend funds for *Women's Weekly* once Xiang stepped down from its editorship, and it ceased publication soon after.

The Mobilization of Women in Guangdong

After the successful Nationalist military campaigns in 1924, Guangdong became a revolutionary center. For many people, participating in political life became routine, and the city was dubbed the "Red Canton" by *Western Journal* (Gilmartin 1995,152). Women's emancipation issues were integrated into this revolutionary political culture and strongly promoted by the new government's commitment to gender reform. Women's issues were inserted into publications, theaters, and the celebrations of revolutionary holidays. Memorial meetings were held on the anniversaries of the death of the famous woman leader of the German socialist party, Rosa Luxemburg, whose image represented the ideal of women's emancipation: revolutionary virtue, commitment, and self-sacrifice.

The Central Women's Department was established in 1924, and He Xiangning, the wife of Liao Zhongkai (one of the most powerful leaders in the Nationalist Party), headed this department. The CCP sent a group of its women leaders down to Guangzhou, including two high-ranking Communist women, Deng Yingchao and Cai Chang. They were assigned to work in He Xiangning's department (Cai as the secretary in the Central Women's Department, Deng as the secretary of the Guangdong Provincial Women's Department). Deng was well known in women's circles for her articles about women's issues and as a founding member of the May Fourth Awakening Society in Tianjin, among other positions. Cai was the sister of Cai Hesen and in 1922 married Li Fuchun, who was one of the leading figures of the CCP. (Both Deng and Cai became top leaders in the All China Women's Federation and held high-ranking positions in the CCP after 1949.)

Deng and other young communist women leaders were extremely energetic in their efforts to expand mass women's organizations, with the result that these organizations tilted the political climate in women's circles toward the left. They wanted to politicize gender issues and tried to involve women in the nationalist revolution on this basis. "To them, this meant stressing the potentially divisive issues of free-choice marriage, the right to divorce, and the abolition of concubinage and polygamy" (Gilmartin 1995, 161). Their strategy in women's mobilization was more radical than He Xiangning's moderate one, but both sides managed to coexist in mutually supportive programs.

The National Revolutionary Army under the command of Chiang Kai-shek marched north out of Guangdong in July 1926. This campaign became known as the Northern Expedition, whose purpose was to defeat more than thirty-four warlord forces in order to unify China under one nationalist government. Many women were involved in a variety of auxiliary teams, working as spies, propagandists, nurses, carriers, and grassroots organizers. Some of them were dressed in military uniforms as soldiers, though rarely in direct combat (Gilmartin 1995, 175). Cai Chang served as head of a propaganda team, and she set up a short team-leadership training class for women after the army arrived in Nanchang. Propaganda teams of the Northern Expedition distributed much literature there, distinguishing their treatment of women from that of the warlords. The revolutionary soldiers of the Northern Expedition were presented as defenders of women who wanted to create public roles for women and end female exploitation (181). Hence, the Northern Expedition greatly expanded the mass women's movement into central China's Hubei province.

The United Front of the Nationalist and the Communist parties began to crumble in early 1927. Following the Northern Expedition, Chiang's right wing established a nationalist capital at Nanjing, and he turned against the CCP, sending his troops into Shanghai to arrest and execute Communists. The head of the Wuhan government, Wang Jingwei, announced the Communists' expulsion from the Nationalist Party. Historians gave the purge of the CCP the name of the White Terror (Perkins 1999, 77). Thousands were killed, but some escaped.

Women were not spared from the bloody breakup of the coalition between the CCP and the GMD. "Women's bodies were subject to mutilation as a statement against female activism, which had come to be viewed as a disturbing indicator of a world turned upside down" (Gilmartin 1995, 199). Cai Chang estimated in her talk with Helen Snow that more than one thousand Communist women organizers and leaders were killed during the first year of the White Terror (199). Xiang Jingyu was executed publicly at Wuhan on May 1, 1928, and accused in an official statement in Nationalist newspapers of improper sexual conduct leading to the breakup of her marriage. It insinuated that the most important facet of her political career had been her sexual behavior (212). This marked the end of the expanding mass women's movements by the joint efforts of women leaders of both parties.

Comments on the Struggle for Formal Equality in the May Fourth Era

The foregoing examination of various Chinese feminist approaches reveals that the pursuit of women's equality went through ups and downs in the early twentieth century, when it was supported by both the CCP and the leftists of the GMD. We also see the close links between issues of feminism, nationalism, and communism on Chinese soil. These three social ideals could go side by side in the national crisis of imperialist hegemony and oppression of the Chinese people. However, the Chinese national crisis of survival meant that Chinese feminist movements were not independent. Male leftist nationalists and communists played important roles in awakening women's consciousness to fight for women's emancipation, but they also obstructed women's independent movements by removing women leaders from their positions.

Despite the differences among them, all these approaches shared a common cause in seeking formal equality for women. They all advocated that women should have equality before the law and equal rights and responsibilities of citizenship. Since the idea of formal sex equality emblematized the rebellion against feudal ideology, which intrinsically devalued women, all modern thinkers adopted the model of formal equality in order to win women's support for their own cause, whether it was nationalist or communist. The model of formal equality appearing in nationalist and emerging in communist thoughts was indeed the ground for the two parties' United Front, and especially for the united front and mobilization against oppression and exploitation of women. I will assess the strengths and problems in the pursuit of formal equality using a dialogue of Western feminist challenges to this model.

The strength of formal equality, in my view, is in its equal valuation of men and women. A principle of equal concern and respect for every individual is a commonplace in Western liberalism, but not a familiar language to the Chinese people who in the early twentieth century had a two-thousand-year tradition of Confucianism.

Confucian ethics always focused on the ideas of *ren* and role models of being *ren*, rather than seeking principles of freedom, equality, and individual happiness. The call of formal equality fundamentally challenged a long and unquestioned worship of the traditional ideology. Through the critiques of Confucianism, people in the May Fourth Movement began to see that their only hope in saving the whole nation was to accept democratic arguments against feudal dictatorship and that the only way to liberate women was to accept the value of freedom and equality, which had been wholly ignored in traditional Confucian doctrines. Without this pursuit of formal equality, they could not even begin to think how to change women's inequality and sufferings. Therefore, the model of formal equality is a necessary step in delivering women from their oppression.

What are the shortcomings of the pursuit of formal equality for women? As I illustrated, most of those engaging in the feminist dialogue at the time of the May Fourth Movement emphasized women's right to be treated as politically and morally equal with men. Some views mentioned women's economic independence as vital to their equality. However, these analyses opposing the devaluation of women in the traditional ethics did not go far enough to investigate what it would be like in women's situations if they had formal equal rights. Some classic Western feminist readings expose the weaknesses, limitations, and inconsistencies in the ideal of formal equality.

Mary Wollstonecraft wrote *A Vindication of the Rights of Women* in 1792, arguing that women had the potential for full rationality to carry out moral responsibilities as men did. The fact that women did not always realize this potentiality was due to the fact that they were deprived of education and confined to the domestic sphere (Jaggar 1983, 38). Wollstonecraft also sought to show that reason has no sex, knowledge has no sex, and mind itself is sexless. This point emphasizes the very abstract feature of formal equality. Nevertheless, the abstract point makes her attempt to extend liberal principles of equality to women problematic. As Moira Gatens states: "No matter how strong the power of reason, it cannot alter the fact that male and female embodiment, at least as lived in the eighteenth century, involved vastly different social and political consequences" (Shanley and Pateman 1991, 113). Gatens argues that women's traditional labor is not visible in the public sphere, does not count as socially necessary, and is not acknowledged in any system of public exchange. Thus, without taking seriously the different situations between men and women, the call for the realization of the rights of women by appealing to the model of formal equality is insufficient and fails to reach its goal.[18] However, as noted, Wollstonecraft does indicate the weakness of the concept of formal equality for women and her vision still inspires many contemporary feminists to focus on women's rights and equality by changing the conditions of women's embodiment. Furthermore, from Wollstonecraft's work, feminists realize that women's formal rights are not sufficient for them to achieve equality with men who do not have the same problems as women do under the terms of sexual neutrality.

John Stuart Mill wrote another feminist classic, *On the Subjection of Women*, in 1869. This essay provides one of the nineteenth century's strongest arguments for opening to women opportunities for suffrage, education, and employment. Following a brief argument for "equal rights" Mill gives a thorough critique of the corruption of marital inequality. Although he criticizes the patriarchal family as not being a school of democracy, Mill does not extend his criticism of inequality to the sexual division of labor (Shanley and Pateman 1991, 164).

Mill believes that establishing legal equality in marriage would require men to sacrifice the political, legal, and economic advantages they enjoyed "simply by being born male." He supports such legal rights as women's suffrage, the Married Women's Property Bills, the Divorce Act of 1857, etc. He contends that suffrage would both develop women's faculties through participation in civic decisions and enable married women to protect themselves from male-imposed injustices such as lack of rights to control their income and child custody. Also, he advocates that education and employment equality should give women alternatives to marriage and provide them means of self-support if marriage fails. These formal rights would recognize women's independent personalities and enable them to meet their husbands more nearly as equals (Shanley and Pateman 1991, 170).

However, Mill goes further to insist that the subjection of women cannot be ended by law alone. Besides the law, the reformation of education, of opinion, of social inculcation, of habits, and finally of the conduct of family life itself needs to be accomplished. He points out that men's fear of living with an equal leads them to deny all other occupations to women, but retain marriage as "a law of despotism" (Shanley and Pateman 1991, 170). Thus, in Mill's analysis of family life, the only way for husband and wife to be equal is through friendship. "Mill's final prescription to end the subjection of women was not equal opportunity but spousal friendship; equal opportunity was a means whereby such friendship could be encouraged" (175). Unfortunately, Mill seemed to forget his own warning that women could be imprisoned not only by law but also by informal customs, and he ignored other conditions that might hinder or promote marital friendship. In his discussion of marital equality, he fails to entertain the possibility that shared parenting such as nurturing and caring for children, etc., would contribute to spousal friendship (176).

In a contemporary discussion of formal equality, Robert Nozick in his book, *Anarchy, State, and Utopia*, gives the well-known libertarian defense of formal equality as a necessary and sufficient condition for achieving equality. Nozick defends the classic liberal view of the individual as the ultimate unit of moral worth. According to him, a respect for individuality and distinctiveness dictates that people be given the freedom to pursue their life plans unless those actions interfere with the freedom of others to pursue their life plans (Koggel 1998, 73). However, Nozick takes the removal of formal barriers to be both necessary and sufficient for achieving equality, and in doing so he discounts the relevance of differences in initial starting positions. Koggel objects, "But an examination of the agents and their starting positions would appear to be highly relevant to an assessment of whether equal opportunity actually obtains" (75).

According to Koggel's point, it is unjust that people who face different obstacles in initial starting positions, such as lack of income for training or for proper nutrition, end up with unequal opportunities. Hence, an adequate conception of equality must pay attention to the obstacles affecting some people but not others, women but not men, the poor but not the rich. Those obstacles are always less visible and more intransigent than formal barriers and thus more difficult to remove (75).

Through all the above challenges to the classic liberal theory of formal equality of opportunity, it is obvious that the main failure of formal equality as a conception of sex equality is its blindness to women's different situations. Under the guise of formal equality, women could obtain all legal rights that men hold, but still remain dependent on their husbands; their inferior position would remain unchanged. Therefore, it is insufficient merely to remove formal barriers and leave informal obstacles untouched.

I argue that the Chinese patriots during the May Fourth era badly needed a new theory for a united China and the survival of all her people. Liberal thought and the idea of democracy were necessary and useful as radical tools against corrupted feudal ideologies of Confucianism, and liberal feminism was welcome in other theories of the national, Marxist, or socialist movements. The mixture of feminism and communism in Xiang and others, and their extraordinary contribution to feminist movements and women's mobilization, reflected the interdependent relations between feminism, nationalism, and communism. Considering the violent and turbulent situations of warlord conflicts, any ideal theories would crumble in practice. The nationalists and communists realized that the liberal idea of democracy and formal equality for women could be used as a radical means, rather than a deep value, to their own ends. Thus, it was impossible for those who had a mixture of these three philosophies to further investigate the different situations between men and women and differences among women in the application of formal equality for women. I would say that the women's revolutionary movements for seeking formal equality during the May Fourth era were the best and necessary beginning to opposing their oppression, but women were so vulnerable in the systematic sexist society that they were easily suppressed by the brutal violence and unjust treatment in male-dominated thinking.

It is obvious that the supposed male feminists in fact controlled "their" women tightly. For instance, women's formal membership remained a problem in the history of the CCP (see Gilmartin 1995, 104-5). Xiang, Wang, and Gao, whose memberships were of nebulous status, were considered as natural and automatic extensional members of their husbands. No matter how significantly they played their roles in the revolutionary events, these women were only "informal power holders" (104) and their positions changed if their marriage status changed. One way in which the CCP controlled the relations between feminism and Communism was by putting female Communist feminists in secondary status. Women were not fully in charge of their own movement at all.

In conclusion, the May Fourth Movement inspired by the liberal theory of formal equality inaugurated a Chinese Renaissance that promised a new hope for Chinese women's emancipation. The male communist feminists made contributions to women's rights and emancipation movements, though they were not immune from the existing gender hierarchy at that time. The female nationalist and communist feminists devoted themselves completely to the cause of the women's movement, and they associated consciously with other groups of women based on women's issues.

Women's first striving for their rights and equality went side by side with the earliest Chinese pursuit of democracy, and without the alluring flag of democracy women's issues could not be raised in public discussions. Unfortunately, although the pursuit of women's emancipation and equality continued in the arenas of the CCP, the turbulent situation and wars during the 1920s put out the fire of democracy and suppressed independent women's movements. In the absence of democracy, progress toward women's equality was extremely limited.

Notes

1. The Reform Movement of 1898; also known as the Hundred Days Reform, a series of social and institutional reforms by Qing emperor Guangxu during the 103 days from June 11 to September 21, 1898. The goal of the reform was to end government corruption, which angered the Manchu members in Qing court. Empress Dowager Cixi sup-

pressed the reform, arrested the emperor, and executed all reformers except Kang and Liang, who escaped to Japan.

2. In this book, the New May Fourth refers to the demonstration by students in Tian An Men Square in 1989.

3. The Opium War (1839-1842) was initiated by Great Britain to force China to open up to the Western system of trade. China ceded Hong Kong to Britain with a 99-year lease and Hong Kong peacefully reverted to China in 1997. See Dorothy Perkins, *Encyclopedia of China* (New York: Round Table Press, 1999), 368-69.

4. Hu, Shi (Hu Shih; 1891-1962) was a famous educator, philosopher, and diplomat. He studied under John Dewey at Columbia University before 1917 and became a professor of philosophy at Beijing University during the May Fourth Movement. See Dorothy Perkins (1999), 218-19.

5. Chen, Duxiu (Chen Tu-hsiu; 1879-1942) was a founder and leader of the Chinese Communist Party and served as the first secretary of the CCP from 1921 to 1927. Mao deposed Chen and removed him from the party in 1927. See Dorothy Perkins (1999), 64-65.

6. The Communist International, or Comintern, under the will of Lenin, aided GMD with the purpose of helping the growing communist movement in China. The Sun-Joffe agreement of January 27, 1923, provided support to the GMD with weapons, equipment, and supplies. The Soviet Union also sent advisors to instruct and train Chinese cadets in Soviet methods in the Whampoa Academy. At the first congress of the GMD in January 1924, seven communists were elected to the Central Committee of GMD and to seven other key posts. But the communists were excluded from units under Chiang's command after Sun's death (1925), and the GMD split into left and right. See Thornton, *China, A Political History—1917-1980*, (1982).

7. Lu Xun (Lu Hsun; 1881-1936) was the first Chinese author of modern novels and the first major Chinese author to write in the vernacular. He wrote stories of the highest quality, concentrating on the social and political conflicts in China during the warlord period (1916-1928). He was a founder of the China Freedom League and the China League of Left-wing Writers. See Dorothy Perkins (1999), 297-98.

8. Lu, Xun, "My Views on Chastity" (1918), in All China Women's Federation (ACWF), Unit of History of Women's Movement, *Wusi Shiqi FunuWenti Wenxuan (Selected Writings on Women's Issues during the May Fourth Period)* (Beijing: Shenghuo Dushu Xinzhi Sanlian Shudian, 1981), 115-123.

9. Wu Yu, "On Filial Piety," (1920) in ACWF 1981, 155-59.

10. Li and Chen co-founded the Chinese Communist Party, and Li's most important function was to develop political theory for the Communists. He was a leader of the May Fourth Movement of 1919, and a professor of history at the prestigious Beijing University. He was executed by the warlord in Beijing in 1927. See Dorothy Perkins (1999), 274-75.

11. Li Daozhao, "Women's Liberation and Democracy" (1919), in ACWF 1981, 95.

12. Li Daozhao, "Women's Liberation and Democracy" (1919), in ACWF 1981, 26-27.

13. Li Daozhao, "Women's Issues after War" (1919), in ACWF 1981, 19-20.

14. Chen Duxiu, "Women's Issues and Socialism" (1921), in ACWF 1981, 80-83.

15. Xiang Jingyu, "On Women's Liberation and Reformation" (1920), in ACWF 1981, 68-73.

16. Mao Dun (Mao Tun; 1896-1981) was a famous modern Chinese novelist and pioneer of China's revolutionary culture. He played an active role in the May Fourth Movement and became one of the earliest members of the Chinese Communist Party. See Dorothy Perkins (1999), 310.

17. Ding Ling (Ting Ling; 1904-1986) was the best-known modern Chinese woman writer, the chief editor of *The Dipper*, the official journal of the Left-wing League for seven years. See Dorothy Perkins (1999).

18. Moira Gatens, "The Oppressed State of My Sex: Wollstonecraft on Reason, Feeling and Equality," in *Feminist Interpretations and Political Theory*, ed. Mary Lyndon Shanley and Carole Pateman (University Park: Pennsylvania State University Press, 1991), 112-28.

Chapter Three

Women's Equality in Mao's Time

Among those male feminist thinkers during the May Fourth Movement, Mao Zedong was the most radical and enthusiastic advocate of women's equality. In this chapter, I will examine Mao's view of women's equality: his view of women's emancipation after the 1920s and his late view of women's substantive equality in production from 1956 to 1976. Then, I will discuss and assess the strength and weakness of Mao's view of substantive equality for women with a focus on his class reduction of gender issues. I will argue that Mao's so-called democratic centralism consolidated his subjective line of thinking and led to his authoritarian method to suppress women's independent voices on their own equality.

Mao (1893-1976) saved the main forces of the Red Army by his successful military strategy against Chiang Kai-shek's fifth "encirclement and suppression" campaign around the Red area in Kiangsi (Jiangxi) in 1934. He became the number one leader of the Political Bureau of the Chinese Communist Party (CCP) and the military forces, during the Zunyi Conference on the Long March of the Red Army, in January of 1935 (Schram 1989, 52). Gradually, Mao's thought, philosophy, and reputation spread all over the country and represented the dominant and only authority of the party, the military, and the state after the CCP won the GMD (Guomindang Party) and unified China during the 1950s. It was undisputed in China from 1956 to 1976 that although the most important policies should be made by the CCP, only Mao had the final decision regarding them. Mao's thought, theory, and policies were the soul and principles of the party and government, and his words about women were the authority and criterion that guided the party's concrete policies for women. All women's federations at every level did their best to implement and supervise the practice of those policies. Mao's view of women's emancipation and his criticism of the old ideologies (Confucianism, feudalism, superstitions, customs) that advocated the subordination of women revealed a view of women that both represented Marxist principles and introduced some distinctive Maoist characteristics. That is, although he followed the Marxist analysis in regarding women as the first oppressed class and attributed their oppression to economic reasons, Mao also analyzed women's issues in a deeper way and posited reasons other than economic ones for women's subordination. Particularly, he regarded women as a special group, the most oppressed under the Chinese feudal system, the most in need of revolution, and the most reliable in the Chinese revolution during the wars and in the socialist construction after a new China was established in 1949.

Most Chinese women in Mao's time would acknowledge his great concern for promoting their position in society and would show great respect for Mao's thought and policy. Without the party's policy of women's equality, expressed in the slogans of "Women hold up half the sky!" and "Women can do everything men can!" women could not have entered the public world to seek economic independence and political equality. However, most women met many problems in their lives under the party's policy of gender equality: they were not equal to the men in their family or to their colleagues in the workplace. Most women had double shifts and burdens when they participated in production. There were many issues regarding gender discrimination in society, but these issues could not be raised with Mao's emphasis on class struggle and his dominant theory of continuing revolution under the dictatorship of the proletariat. Late in his leadership, Mao tried to seize supreme power and strongest control of the party, and his view of women as a single voice suppressed women's different voices. Women could not even express their opinions about gender issues that reduced to class analysis or make any mention of differences between class oppression and gender oppression. Mao never distinctly addressed them as separate issues. Mao's most important political thought was the theory of continuity of the revolution under the dictatorship of the proletariat, and he took class struggle as the key link in everything, which led to his serious mistake of expanding class struggle[1] into all social and personal issues.

Mao's View of Women's Emancipation After the May Fourth Movement

After the May Fourth Movement, Mao's political thought changed, and he became a Marxist in 1920 (Snow 1992, 116). Mao then insisted on the basic principles of Marxism and applied these theories to the Chinese revolution. During the democratic revolution period from 1920 to 1948, Mao viewed peasants, who occupied almost 90 percent of the population, as the main force of the revolution and the rural area as the revolutionary base. He continued to criticize the old ideology among the peasants and called them and other groups of people to unite together against the "three mountains" of oppression—imperialism, feudalism, and bureaucratic capitalism—to build a new China. From 1920 to 1948, the Communist Party and the Guomindang Party experienced the formation and dissolution of two separate unions (first from 1924 to 1927; second from 1937 to

1945). Finally, Mao and the CCP won the war with the support of great masses and a new China was established in 1949.

In the period of the democratic revolution, Mao realized that orthodox Marxist class analysis could not properly apply to the situation of women's oppression. Oppression seemed common to all Chinese women across all classes and some upper-class women from wealthy families ran away from their oppressive situations to join the revolution in Soviet base areas during the war. Two of their reasons for joining the revolution were the CCP policies of freedom to select one's marriage partner and of equality between men and women. Following are comparisons between the policies of the Red Army and the CCP, and the GMD, as cited in *Women in Modern China*. These comparisons clearly show why many women, including upper-middle-class women, supported the CCP and the Red Army:

Comparing Views toward Women: Guomindang [G] and Communist [C]
    1. Leader's Views:
[G]: None of Chiang's "Eight Principles" deal specifically with women.
[C]: Mao Zedong had written a series of articles in 1919 on the condition of women. In later writings he also mentioned the need for women's equality.
    2. Attitudes toward Revolutionary Women of 1920s:
[G]: Allowed the killing of Communist women, approximately 1,000. The number of women who were raped but not killed is not known.
[C]: The party was severely hurt by the attack, and the remaining women and men were very bitter. They claimed some women were merely teachers and students, not Party members.
    3. Marriage and Property Laws:
1931 Guomindang Code:
a. Patriarchal family abolished; b. No arranged marriages; c. Father keeps the child in case of divorce; d. Adultery is punishable for both men and women; e. No official concubinage; f. Women could inherit property; g. Father's family gets custody of child if both parents dead; h. Both husband and wife own goods, but husband manages them.
1930 Communist Code:
a. Patriarchal family abolished; b. No forced marriages; c. Divorce is available for both men and women; d. No legitimate/illegitimate children; e. Polygamy prohibited; f. Marriages had to be registered.
    4. Enforcement of Laws:
[G]: No registration of marriage; no major attempt to inform peasants of law changes; urban people followed new laws more.
[C]: Began enforcing in 1930 in Jiangxi and later in Soviet Yenan. Some appearance of attempted enforcement, how deep, not yet known.
    5. Ideology and Philosophy:
[G]: The New Life Movement stressed "Propriety, Justice, Honesty, and Self Respect." The Eight Principles of the "New Life" did not specifically mention women.
[C]: Marxist-Leninist philosophy stressed the equality of women.

    6. Education:
[G]: Military training for boys, nurse's training for girls. "Girls and boys need separate training." Senior girls took care of younger students; boys practiced as clerks, telephone men. However, women's groups worked against infanticide, foot binding, and slavery.
[C]: Some training courses for women in leadership technique; mostly co-educational but some special classes in literacy for women. Groups worked against infanticide, foot binding, and slavery.
(Bingham and Gross 1980, 62)

The specific contribution of the CCP to the women's movements was its emphasis on organizing groups of women, training women cadres, and establishing women's sections (later called women's federations) in all districts. The women's cause was closely linked with the cause of the CCP, and it was difficult to determine which of the three areas of struggle should be prioritized: women's rights, class revolution, or the nation's liberation. Mao investigated these issues in some rural districts and his view of women during this period seemed ambiguous, but it can be expressed in three points as Kang Keqing[2] wrote in her article, "Chairman Mao Leads Us to the Road of Complete Emancipation of Women": 1. Women are a decisive force in the success or failure of the revolution; 2. Only the victory of the oppressed class can bring about the real emancipation of women; 3. Mao is greatly concerned for women's needs and interests.[3] These three aspects of Mao's view of women are generally true, but from the standpoint of feminist thinking, these views should be challenged by the idea of what really matters in gender oppression: Can the Chinese revolution solve all women's issues? Should women continue to explore "women's issues" after the revolution?

Mao's Great Concern for Women's Needs

Mao always expressed great sympathy and special concern for women's concrete problems, and he issued many documents to help women solve their problems and to make women's life easier in their double workload. Nevertheless, similar to what the CCP leaders did in the May Fourth Movement, Mao did not allow women's organizations to make any decisions about women's policy separate from the party's policy.
    Early in 1932, Mao issued a special proposal concerning how to improve the life of women in the Soviet base area, and in 1934 Mao issued a report explaining the new marriage code of the Soviet government (the CCP government). Mao stated:

> The oppression of women is much harder than men's because of the savagery of the marriage relation for thousands of years. Therefore,

the present marriage law of the Soviet government must pay special attention to protecting women's benefits in the case of divorce and men must shoulder their half of the obligations. (ACWF 1988, 43)

This code is the preceding structure for the first marriage law in 1951 of the People's Republic of China, which prescribes that men and women can get married according to their agreement and can divorce through one side's request.

Mao was also concerned about women's procreative health and about birth control. During the domestic war (1920s and 1930s) Mao allocated five silver yuan (the Chinese currency unit) from the very limited money of the Red Army to every pregnant woman comrade for her nutrition. In 1942, Mao specifically mentioned in a conference on economic and financial issues that there were many women whose feet were still being bound, and he declared: "We should use both propaganda and legal enforcement to wipe out this habit within a short time. From now on, no one can be allowed to bind young girls' feet" (ACWF 1988, 56). This call finally ended the brutal feudal custom in the lives of Chinese women.

Only the Victory of the Oppressed Class Can Bring About the Real Emancipation of Women

Why are women the most oppressed? How can they gain their emancipation? Marxist class theory, when applied to women's issues, explained that class exploitation was the origin of women's oppression. Therefore, the only way to obtain liberation for women was to end class exploitation. For this end to be achieved, women needed to participate in productive activities to gain economic independence and create the proper conditions for the complete emancipation of women. In Frederick Engels's *The Origin of the Family, Private Property, and the State*, this view is expressed as follows:

> The first class opposition that appears in history coincides with the development of the antagonism between man and woman in monogamous marriage, and the first class oppression coincides with that of the female sex by the male. (Engels 1993, 129)

When Engels explains why a mother's right was overthrown, he mentions two reasons: "as wealth increased it made the man's position in the family more important than the woman's" and consequently it "created an impulse to exploit this strengthened position in order to overthrow, in favor of his children, the traditional order of inheritance" (1993, 119). It seems that Engels attributed women's oppression to economic reasons. There remains an unexplainable question. "As to how and when this revolution took place among prehistoric times, we have no knowledge" (120). According to Alison Jaggar's criticism, there seems to be a theoretical gap in the Marxist analysis of women's oppression. In her book, *Feminist Politics and Human Nature*, Jaggar points out that so far as it goes, it seems to indicate that Engels believed that women were not systematically exploited and degraded in pre-class societies, but that such systematic subjugation occurred with the introduction of class society. However, there exists some evidence that even in pre-class societies women were not entirely equal to men.

> It is interesting that Engels himself even provides some of this evidence. For instance, in his discussion of pairing marriage which, he claims, occurred during a period when women were still equal or even superior to men, Engels remarks that the capture and purchase of women began at this time. He attributes this development to a shortage of women, although he never explains why women should become scarce with the advent of pairing marriage. Whatever the reasons for this shortage, it should be obvious immediately that persons who are being captured and purchased are not the equals of those who are doing the capturing and purchasing. (Jaggar 1983, 73)

If women were not equal to men before the transformation to class society, there should be some reasons for women's subjugation rather than only an economic explanation. Yet, this unnoticed aspect of women's oppression was left out from the Marxist theory of women's oppression and liberation. Mao also remained uncertain about the root of women's oppression and only encouraged women to unite with other groups of people in the struggle for national liberation. Nevertheless, Mao had already touched on the hard part of this root: not only the economic element, but also other reasons such as men's immorality, women's reproductive responsibilities, and unreasonable social arrangements.

Women as a Decisive Force in the Success of the Chinese Revolution

Mao did not think that the success of the Russian Revolution of 1917, which had been carried out by industrial workers and intellectuals, could be emulated in China, because any plan for a new China must actively involve peasants, who made up four-fifths of China's population. But the advice of the Communist Comintern ignored the peasants. Mao returned to Hunan to investigate the progress of the peasant movement there since he had left his post to work as a lecturer in the School for the Peasants' Movement at Guangzhou.

In his "Investigation of the Peasant Movement in Hunan," Mao pointed out that a man in China is usually subjected to the domination of three systems of authority, that is, the state system (political authority), the clan system (clan authority), and the supernatural system (religious authority). As for women, Mao said:

[I]n addition to being dominated by these three systems of authority, they are also dominated by the men (the authority of the husband). These four authorities—political, clan, religious, and masculine—are the embodiment of the whole feudal-patriarchal system and ideology, and are the four thick ropes binding the Chinese people, particularly the peasants. (Mao 1967, 1:44)

Among these four authorities, the crucial one is the political, so the first task is to overthrow the political authority of the landlords in the countryside, which is the backbone of all the other systems. As to the authority of husband, Mao believed:

[T]his has always been weaker among the poor peasants because, out of economic necessity, their womenfolk have to do more manual labor than the women of the richer classes and therefore have more say and greater power of decision in family matters. With the increasing bankruptcy of the rural economy in recent years, the basis for men's domination over women has already been weakened, with the rise of the peasant movement, the women in many places have now begun to organize rural women's associations; the opportunity has come for them to lift up their heads, and the authority of the husband is getting shakier every day. In a word, the whole feudal patriarchal system and ideology is tottering with the growth of the peasants' power. (Mao 1967, 1:46)

According to Mao, the task in 1927 was to lead the peasants to put their greatest efforts into the political struggle to overthrow the authority of landlords. The economic struggle should follow immediately, so that the land problem and the other economic problems of the peasants might be solved. At that time, the power of landlords was both political and economic, for most landlords were involved in both local government and local militant forces which would protect their economic interests. Thus, the first task for the party was to organize peasants to overthrow the landlords' control and to redistribute their property among the poor peasants. As for the clan system, superstition, and inequality between men and women, Mao said, "their abolition will follow as a natural consequence of victory in the political and economic struggles" (Mao 1967, 1:46). Here Mao did not give the reason why abolition should follow "naturally." It seemed that the peasants would fiercely oppose anything the landlords advocated, such as feudal customs. The party's policy would be "Draw the bow without shooting, just indicate the motion" (46). Once in action, the peasants would cast aside the idols and pull down the temples to the martyred virgins and the arches to the chaste and faithful widows.

Nevertheless, there was no argument to explain why these actions would follow consequently and in a natural way. In Hunan, Mao called upon the party to put the political task first; otherwise, he believed, the second or third tasks would become an excuse (such as "the peasants' association is destroying religion" and "the peasants' association stands for the communization of wives") to undermine the peasant movement. In Mao's analysis, he found that some peasants opposed the code of freedom of divorce because "it is obvious that they are afraid of losing the labor force in their family" (ACWF 1988, 34). Here we see that Mao placed women's liberation second in order to prioritize ending the feudal relation between the peasants and the landlord. Mao focused his attention on what he saw as the main problem and temporarily put the others aside. This was a political strategy to win the peasants' support for the party.

According to the Marxist theory of class struggle, wherever the phenomenon of oppression remains, resistance will arise, and the greater the oppression, the greater the revolt. Mao also believed that women would be the main force in the Chinese revolution, because of their extreme oppressed status, but there was some contradiction in his view, for gender oppression and class oppression are not the same thing. Mao had already pointed out in his "Investigation of the Peasant Movement in Hunan" that the husband's authority had always been weaker among the poor peasants. It seemed that Mao mixed these two kinds of oppressions or treated them as parallel rather than as antagonistic. Thus, later Mao could claim that only national liberation and class liberation could bring about women's liberation. Mao wrote for the Ninth Party Congress of the Fourth Red Army in December of 1929: "Women comprise one-half of the population. Their poor economic position and extreme oppressed status are not only the evidence of their urgent need of revolution but also the indication of their being the determining force that will win the revolution" (ACWF 1988, 30).

When he called for women's equality, Mao seemed to include all women as a homogeneous group rather than only working class and peasant women. Mao made an enthusiastic call in his speech at the Memorial Meeting to Celebrate March Eighth Women's Day at Yenan in 1940: "Strive for the freedom and equality of women over the whole country!"

> Our women fellows are not only humiliated by Japanese invaders, despots, etc., but also by the uncivilized Chinese men. Women are not allowed to participate in meetings or to speak, to talk about their freedom and equality, or to do things for their own needs. All of these are incorrect. (ACWF 1988, 49)

Mao encouraged all women of the nation to unite and to struggle for their freedom and equality. "We are preparing for another ten years in which to resolve all problems, to wipe out all the roots of pain and to win women's final liberation" (ACWF 1988, 49). Mao made it clear that the miserable situation of women caused by foreign invaders and their oppressed position caused by Chinese men were interrelated. Imperialism, landlords, the feudal system, and the old ideology would be the common enemy of all people including women. The task of overthrowing the three mountains of oppression was necessary and more important than a single struggle for women's rights. Furthermore, the party firmly and simultaneously advocated both the aims of national liberation and women's liberation. Thus, most women agreed with the party's policy and made great contributions to implement these policies.

During the war with Japan (1936-1945), when men were deployed to the front lines, the role of women in production was necessary and critical as they replaced the men (usually their husbands) in production. The Chinese revolution needed the support of women, and women also wanted to change their status. Women had more say through their social participation, and they were particularly active in taking part in revolutionary work. In the Soviet areas,[4] women's congresses were more concerned with the general cause of the Soviet than they were with the specific demands of women. The topics discussed by the congresses included enlarging the Red Army, aid to the Red Army, looking after the dependents of Red Army soldiers, learning to plow, and selling jewelry to buy government bonds. In order to obtain victory for the whole nation, women were willing to sacrifice all their belongings, even their lives.[5] Mao had predicted in 1939 at the opening ceremony of Yenan Women's College: "The day when women of the whole country rise up will be the day of victory for the Chinese revolution."[6] It was quite true that women played an important role in the success of the Chinese revolution. The revolution greatly increased women's liberation, but could it completely accomplish women's liberation? Did gender matter after the revolution had been won?

After the White Terror of 1927, Mao became more and more emphatic about national liberation under the leadership of the CCP. The different policies on women that we see in the chart comparing views of the GMD and the CCP toward women indicated that the CCP was more reliable in leading women to fight for their liberation and equality. Although Mao's analysis of women as the most oppressed class was vague because he did not give a detailed analysis about how class and gender oppressions work together against women, he was always an enthusiastic supporter of women's needs and interests.

As we see, many women's issues were linked with the serious national situation (tangled warfare between the warlords and the dangers of foreign aggression). It was reasonable for Mao to develop his view of women and to pay greater attention to linking women's liberation with national liberation. During the 1930s and 1940s, the CCP and the Red Army went through the arduous experience of carrying on the revolutionary cause and they achieved significant development of the military, production, and the government under Mao's leadership. Mao's thought and strategies became more and more authoritarian in the lives of the party and people in the revolutionary base.

The next section will examine Mao's late view of women's equality in production.

Mao's Late View of Women's Equality in Production

From 1949 to 1976, Mao gradually developed his theory of continuing revolution under the dictatorship of the proletariat, and this influenced his view of women and of the party's policy regarding women. There was no doubt that women's social position had changed fundamentally. According to statistical information in *Funuxuegailun*,[7] the percentage of women's participation in paid employment in the entire nation in 1949 was only 7.5 percent and the percentage by 1956 was up to 13.48 percent. The average annual rise in the rate of employment during this period was 15 percent and the rate for women was 23.7 percent. According to information from the State Statistics Bureau published in the *People's Daily* of October 12, 1994, one-third of the women in China were employed by 1980. Although this number still shows the uneven status between men and women, it does represent a fundamental improvement in the status of women in new China as compared to the old society.

According to Mao, women would no longer be the slaves of men if they could gain economic independence through paid jobs legally guaranteed by party policies and the law. The inequality of men and women was changing rapidly due to many state-supported social programs that greatly benefited women, such as free medical care for women and children, child care centers and kindergartens in most local districts, and paid maternity leave for childbirth and breastfeeding. The number of women cadres or women who held positions of responsibility in the party expanded after 1950. If we take the number of female delegates to the eighth (1956) through the tenth (1973) Chinese Communist Party's Congress and female members of the central committees as examples, female membership comprised almost 5 percent to 10 percent (the total female number was 4 out of 97 members in the eighth and was 20 out of 195 in the tenth).[8] This was far from satisfactory, but it shows the improvements gained by women in political participation. All of these advances were due to Mao's leadership and the state policies. Mao's later view (1949-1970s) of women is expressed in his speeches, inscriptions, poems, essays, and slogans. Some of his slogans became very famous and were commonly used, such as "Women can hold up half the sky!" "Women can do everything men can," and "Chinese women love military training more than makeup!" These ideas had a profound effect on the lives of Chinese women during the 1950s, 1960s, and the 1970s. Chinese women legally gained equal rights in 1950, and women's legal equality was guaranteed for the first time by the Constitution of 1950. Through the party's protection and advocacy, more women participated in the workplace and in farmwork under the policy of equal pay for equal work. Compared with that of their older foot-bound sisters, the social position of women had improved significantly both economically and ideologically. Mao states:

In order to build a great socialist society, it is of the utmost importance to arouse the broad masses of women to join in the activity of
production. Men and women must receive equal pay for equal work
in production. Genuine equality between the sexes can only be realized in the process of the socialist transformation of society as a
whole. (Mao 1966, 297)

Many people believed that Chinese women had achieved complete liberation. However, some women held a different opinion. They believed that women
still had many special problems in their private lives, and their needs and interests were being obscured by slogans proclaiming women's equality. I will discuss these problems under the following three headings: (1) Problems in equal
pay for equal work; (2) Women's double burden; (3) Did women have independent organizations?

Problems in Equal Pay for Equal Work

Although Mao and the party repeatedly claimed credit for the equal pay policy
(Mao in ACWF 1988, 64; 1966, 297 and 298), practical problems existed when
women's work was evaluated in the brigade production. For example, women's
working points were much lower than men's when they worked shoulder to
shoulder in the same field and for the same number of hours; typically, a young
man would get 10 points if he worked well but the best woman could only get
7.5 points. This was my experience during the 1970s when I lived in a village in
North Shanxi. I worked very hard with peasant women in the field from 1969 to
1973, and I got the top working points for a woman: 7.5. The situation was similar in other places, as the author of *Women in Rural China*, Vibeke Hemmel,
stated: "[A] man and a woman obtained different work-points for doing the
same work. The man received ten points, while the woman got only seven"
(1984, 23). Perhaps men could do more work ploughing and harvesting, but
women were much quicker and better in picking and selecting cotton flowers or
other things.

   In the factories and the service front, men and women would get the same
wage if they had the same kind of job. Why was it that women in rural districts
could not get equal pay? It was clear that the standards of working points depended on physical strength. At that time, most people in the countryside lived
in bad conditions, and manual labor was the main productive method. The
evaluation of men's and women's work depended only on their physical
strength; hence, it was rationalized that women should get 7.5 points because of
their physical weakness. The party encouraged women to compete with men on
the level of physical strength and warned certain cadres not to look down on
women. Because of general assumptions of women's weakness, although some

women could reach a man's standard of physical performance, they did not get the same points as men did.

One of the major obstacles to being equal with men was the sexual division of labor in the home. For example, in my village, women normally left work earlier than men in order to get home to cook and to have dinner ready for the returning men. The women also had more days off every month, especially during the winter season, not for rest, but to do all the housework that had accumulated, such as washing, sewing, and salting the vegetables. "This meant that the men did not count on women as a stable labor power and would therefore not agree to give them as many work points as they got themselves" (Hemmel 1984, 24). The model for women established by the party was "iron girl." It was reported that there was an "iron girl team" in Da Zhai Brigade, Shanxi province, during the middle of the 1970s, which was one of the two red flags in the industry front and the agricultural front; according to Mao, the whole country should learn from them. Nevertheless, in the peasants' mind, the standard for a good girl and a wife was not that of an iron girl who could compete with a man physically, but a good seamstress, a good cook, or a good household manager. The place of women was still regarded to be domestic labor. The social expectations and pressure for women did not encourage them to match the standards established by men.

Women's Double Burden

Although Mao and the party greatly encouraged vast masses of women to take part in production and political activity to improve their economic and political status, in reality, the situation for women remained problematic. Women received lower pay than men in collective production in rural areas and were evaluated as less important than men. Thus, peasant families were willing to send boys to school and keep girls at home to be household helpers. Female infanticide still existed, and asking for bride money was a popular custom, especially in poor districts. Though women workers received equal pay for equal work in factories, vast numbers of women were less educated and thus held less-skilled jobs and received lower pay compared to men as a social group.

Mao exhorted, "Women can hold up half the sky!" In fact, under this slogan, women were required to hold up twice as much of the sky as men, because they had to do all of the domestic labor after a full day's work outside. These double shifts made women less able to compete with their male colleagues for promotion. In any case, the government evaluated and promoted employees by their achievements at work, not by their double responsibilities. Could women work only one job as men did? Could women remain single without family burdens? It seemed that it would be difficult for a family to maintain a living wage if the wife remained at home. For instance, if only one parent worked to raise a family that had more than three children, the family would be too poor to meet its daily needs. During the 1950s and 1960s, after the war against the United States in North Korea early in 1950, most families had four children or more because the party encouraged women to have more children to ensure a large number of socialists. It was necessary for most families to find several jobs in order to earn more. Many urban women and housewives organized and ran small street factories or neighborhood mills to produce handicrafts or other handmade things. One reason for women not to remain single was the shortage of housing. A single woman could not get a room allocated by her working unit during that time, and unmarried people had to share one room with others in their dormitory buildings. Even if a single woman had a room with her parent family, she was stigmatized and lived under social pressure because she was different from others. The National Federation also addressed the so-called socialist morality, that is, the "Five Goods" pointed out by Zhang in her report at the Third National Congress. The argument for thrifty household management went as follows:

> If the family is well run those of its members who are taking part in socialist construction do not look back over their shoulders, but devote themselves wholeheartedly to raising production; if the house is badly run this will influence their production and thus the fulfillment of the state and the co-operatives' plans to raise output. A very large proportion of the articles needed in daily life produced in our country is consumed within the family and the degree of economy practiced by families has a great influence on the national supply of consumer resources . . . Thus thrifty household management can greatly promote an increase in the national production and can promote the national, collective, and family interests. (ACWF 1979, 124-25)

Nevertheless, everything that these workers' dependents did wholeheartedly was only considered an indirect contribution to socialist construction according to this argument. Furthermore, Zhang called on all women to carry out Chairman Mao's instruction of building up the country economically, and as a guideline she emphasized that among the many forms of thrift management—thriftily run factories, thriftily run cooperatives, and thriftily run causes—"we women have the more important responsibility for thrifty household management" (ACWF 1979, 118). In a word, women must hold up the whole sky of the family and half the sky of public jobs. But, if women should first of all manage all of the household work, Mao had no argument in support of his famous slogan: "Women can do everything men can."

From the above discussion, we see that inequality between women and men still existed and that women suffered from these perplexing problems. Mao's slogan, "Women can hold up half the sky," in reality, was difficult to carry out, and Mao simply attributed the difficulties of women's liberation to the influence of traditional ideologies and considered ideological struggles as essentially a class struggle and reduced gender issues into class analysis.

Did Women Have Independent Organizations?

At the Tenth Plenary of the Chinese Communist Party's Eighth Central Committee in 1962, Mao Zedong initiated the slogan, "Never forget the class struggle." This was the signal for the Socialist Education movement that was carried out mainly in rural areas from 1962 to 1965. The movement reached a climax in the middle of the 1960s in the Great Proletarian Cultural Revolution (1966-1976). During these two periods we see that a keen ideological and political battle occurred between Mao's group and the group of Liu Shaoqi (the Chairman of the People's Republic of China) who was accused of "rich-peasant policy" to promote free markets.

Another battle that more directly affected the question of women's equality concerned the continuation of class struggle in the socialist society. As late as 1964, one of the leading theoretical workers, Feng Ding, was criticized for maintaining that the history of society was not the history of class struggle but of man's search for happiness. The question of happiness was a major preoccupation during this period and was the subject of a debate in the Women's Federation paper. The masses of women were not able to see the connection between the question of happiness and Mao's slogan, "Never forget the class struggle," until the famous theorist Feng was criticized. In 1964 the question was raised about the consciousness of women both as members of their sex and as members of different classes. This topic for discussion was criticized in *Honqi*.[9] The editorial rejected the primacy of the social division between the sexes in favor of that between the classes. According to the editorial, in different societies, different classes of women have completely different purposes as ideals of life, and different viewpoints of marriage and love, so the conclusion is that there is no abstract woman or abstract man in the world. This editorial urged women to apply a class analysis to their own individual problems and wider problems and to take part in the class struggle between the bourgeoisie and the proletariat. The Women's Federation magazine, *Women of New China,* published two articles, "What Do Women Live For?" and "On What Criteria Should One Choose a Husband?" These were singled out for criticism in July and August 1966 on the grounds that they directed attention toward women's biological and domestic roles and turned women's attention away from political and revolutionary issues, encouraging them to personalize and individualize their problems. The editor of the magazine, Dong Bian, was criticized for being revisionist and was fired from her post in 1966. From that time on, there was no forum for women's free speech and the Women's Federation became more careful in their attention to propaganda guidelines of the party.

During the Cultural Revolution there were no separate organizations of women, and the definitions of class terms were expanded to include women. As Elisabeth Croll described in her book *Feminism and Socialism in China*:

> The primarily feminist viewpoint was accorded to the bourgeois class and hence to be struggled against and in this manner the struggle for women's liberation was integrated into the current class struggle. Women were therefore to be encouraged to raise their class-consciousness and to take part in politics. (1978, 310)

The All China Democratic Women's Federation was founded at a congress in Beijing in 1949 in order to ensure that the party's political directives and campaigns were known and carried out among women in the countryside and in urban districts. During the 1950s, the cadres of the Women's Federation made contributions to implement the marriage law, to mobilize women, and to awaken their consciousness on women's liberation. In 1957, the Women's Federation held the Third National Congress and changed its name from the All-China Democratic Women's Federation to the National Women's Federation. This congress raised the requirement of Five Goods for women as a standard of a good housewife: (1) thrift and industrious management of the household, (2) unity and mutual aid, (3) child rearing, (4) promotion of public hygiene and health, and (5) study.[10] These requirements were only part of the following three tasks in the working report that Zhang presented to this congress: "Build up the country economically, manage the household thriftily, and strive for socialist construction." Thus, it can be seen that the Women's Federation, on all levels, carried out government and party policy and encouraged women to be good in both the private household sphere and the public paid-labor sphere.

The next congress was not held during the Cultural Revolution until December 1978, twenty-one years after the Third Congress. In 1973, the preparatory meeting for the Fourth National Congress was held and political problems were debated. The criteria for membership in the women's federation were more general than those for specific women's organizations, e.g., (1) diligently study Marxism, Leninism, and Mao's thought, (2) understand the struggle between the revisionist and the revolutionary line, (3) have an unblemished political background, and (4) be actively involved in class struggle, the struggle for production and for scientific experiments.[11] None of these had any direct relevance to the attitudes and the question of women's specific needs and interests. During the 1960s and 1970s, women's organizations had no independent thought or voice. Women were told that they must learn to be diligent and economic in the household as well as in national construction and that they should develop a new socialist morality under the leadership of the party.

In Mao's late view, the most important factor in liberating women was not the material situation but the change in people's minds, the replacement of old ideas by new ones. Mao realized that new thoughts, customs, and culture must appear but there would be a long struggle against the old ones. So Mao said: "Invariably remnants of old ideas reflecting the old system remain in people's minds for a long time and do not easily give way."[12] In order to wipe out the remnants of old ideas that slighted women's roles and advocated male supremacy, Mao launched nationwide ideological campaigns against Lin Biao and Confucius in 1974. Some foreign scholars considered Mao's thought a distinct contribution to Marxism, which called for continuing revolution under the dictatorship of the proletariat,[13] but some Chinese scholars held different opinions.[14] Mao put much stress on the ideological struggle in order to change people's minds and thus moved away from Marxist classical theory, viz. historical materialism, which puts more stress on the economic elements in the transition to a communist society. Class struggle became the overwhelming task in China's transition, which completely ruled out any possibilities of investigating women's double-burden problems.

During the Anti-Confucian movement, women were widely encouraged to rediscover and study their own history with a view to understanding the role of Confucian ideology, its origins, development, and limitations in determining the expectations and self-images of women. Numerous study groups were formed in schools, factories, government institutions, and neighborhoods, and some aimed at combining female students, workers, and peasants together in groups. The *People's Daily* stated that it had been impossible to completely eliminate all of the remnants of Confucian ideology; those advocating male supremacy and the division of labor into domestic and public spheres were the persistent remnants of old habits and customs that underpinned discrimination against women and reflected the influence of the old ruling ideology. Again it was stressed that if women were determined they could identify and criticize the influences of the old ruling ideology, then they would be able to "emancipate their minds, do away with all fetishes and superstitions and press ahead despite the difficulties."[15] As we know, beginning in the 1950s, women were encouraged to take up political study and participate in class struggle and production. The ideological belief that men were superior to women was to be fought at all times. So, the identification of ideological constraints was not a new element introduced in the Anti-Confucian campaign. What was the real purpose of this movement? Croll argues:

> What is significant about the campaign is that it is the most concentrated and analytical attempt to date to integrate the redefinition of the female role into a nationwide effort to change the self-image and expectations of men and women and combine a consciousness of both women's and class interests. (1978, 323)

Through this nationwide study program, great masses of women identified and clarified some important viewpoints, which would greatly affect their role and status. First of all, the historical studies were mainly aimed at drawing attention to the "social origins and class foundations" of the code of ethics which discriminated against women. Women realized through the study program that male supremacy was neither an immutable social principle ordained by heaven nor one dating back to time immemorial, but was a principle developed by Confucius in a specific historical period (during the transition from a slave to a feudal society). Justified by Confucian maxims such as, "Women, like small men, are hard to manage," and "The subordination of women to men is one of the supreme principles of government," ethical codes of subordinated conduct for women were elaborated in the Song dynasty. There was found to be a direct correlation "between the exaltation of Confucius and the degree of subjugation of women." Second, the cruel oppression of women was not due to any biological distinction between men and women, but was rooted in the social system directed by the exploiting classes. Male supremacy was found to be a common feature of societies under the rule of the exploiting classes, be they slave owners, feudal lords, or capitalists. Third, women authors of an article, "On the Historical Confucian Persecution of Women," pointed out that identifying the source of women's oppression was of immense significance in diminishing the remaining influence of Confucius on the position of women (Sun and Lu 1975). Thus, many study groups came to the conclusion that only the demise of Confucian ideology itself would end this resource for manipulation of women by those in positions of political power. Mao believed that change could occur only if ideological origins of the idea of male supremacy were identified and made widely known. The Anti-Confucian campaign by Mao's instructions made a real contribution in helping the great mass of women find the basic Chinese rationale for their oppression.

Perhaps the nationwide movement against Lin Biao and Confucius was influenced by other aspects of the political struggles of that time. In fact, only one tone of criticism was permitted during the whole period of Anti-Confucianism. No debatable ideas or controversial viewpoints were laid out for discussion, and all study groups used one analytical tool: the principle of class analysis as a universal truth to judge who and what should be deemed responsible for women's oppression and subordination. Although ideological constraints were among the main obstacles preventing liberation of women's minds and practices, there were also other elements that prevented women from getting equal social treatment and these should be uncovered.

As we saw earlier, problems with the policy of equal pay for equal work, the double shifts of women, and the devaluation of women all showed that the structural obstacles and ideological obstacles were intertwined and acted to maintain women's subordination. Thus a further redefinition of the role and status of women requires a dual strategy, one that challenges both the economic and ideological obstacles and does not stress one above the other. If only one aspect is emphasized, it fails to address the complexities surrounding the many issues of Chinese women. The Anti-Confucian campaign was designed to draw attention to the convergence of women's interests and class interests, so it stressed only ideological constraints, and as such, equality between men and women was not realized.

I argue that the overwhelming stress on the ideological root of women's oppression imposed by Mao's top-down command had the consequence of suppressing different voices that might have paid attention to other elements preventing women from being equal to men. However, Mao's seizure of supreme control during the Cultural Revolution did not leave any room for a democratic discussion in women's study groups, but only one command voice by centralization of mass opinions. Ironically, Mao utilized the so-called democratic centralism to rationalize his top-down ideology as the best representation of women's interests.

What does Mao mean by democratic centralism? In many places in his writings, he explained the importance of democratic centralism as one of the party's cardinal principles to defeat the enemy. Although he claims that the masses have boundless creative power and inexhaustible enthusiasm for socialism, he believes that the party cannot accept the mass's opinions without centralization. He emphasizes that the party not only needs democracy but also needs centralization even more. In criticizing some comrades favoring mass's opinions one-sidedly, Mao said, "They forget the system of democratic centralism, in which the minority is subordinate to the majority, the lower level to the higher level, the part to the whole and the entire membership to the Central Committee" (1967, 3:44). This is exactly the meaning of "democratic centralism." A party member must take ideas in accordance with the party's line, which in practice meant, no doubt, Mao's political line. From the view of centralism, one should keep Mao's leadership as the only correct party leadership, and this view made Mao absolutely the dominant voice in all issues in China during his reign.

Why was Mao's nondemocratic centralism acceptable in the CCP and used to suppress political dissent? Historically, Mao prioritized the centralized leadership in many political campaigns such as the Yenan Rectification in 1942, the Anti-Rightist Movement in 1957, and finally the Cultural Revolution from 1966 to 1976. During the Chinese democratic revolution before 1956, Mao won the greatest love and worship from the masses, which accounts for the historical success of the CCP under his leadership. This love and loyalty, in return, nurtured the absolute authority of Mao and the party, casting Mao in the image of the infallible leader. Mao came to believe in this image and thought himself the only representative of the highest interests of the people, and their only voice. This authoritarianism, coupled with the party's support, state support, and the blind obedience of the masses, led to the failure of Chinese society, the disaster of the Cultural Revolution, and eventually cast China backward to a dictatorship. Under Mao's dictatorship and dominant voice, women were unable to speak and explore their own burdens. The demands placed on women when they tried to meet the two sets of requirements of public work and family life were overwhelming. They had no idea of how to overcome those contradictions and attain the real emancipation as promised in Mao's teaching that women can do everything men can.

Comments on Mao's View of Women's Equality

Mao's early view on women opened the possibility of investigating the relationship between women's liberation and national and oppressed class liberation, but his late view on women, especially after the 1960s, gradually reduced or closed these possibilities. One of the premises of women's liberation is the nation's independence and democracy, and Mao was correct to link women's liberation to national liberation and to mobilize women to participate in striving for revolution and a new China. However, after this necessary condition was realized and China began its socialist reconstruction, the idea of equality between men and women should have been pursued and practiced in deeper and wider social contexts. During the process of realizing this idea of equality, women's participation, their active involvement and free voices, should have been taken as the decisive element in seeking women's full emancipation. Hence, without independent organization of women and protection for freedom of speech, it was impossible to develop theories and practices that advocated real equality between men and women. Mao's late view on women gradually became a view of predominantly class analysis, reducing gender perspectives to class ideology and eliminating any kind of challenge from the perspective of gender consciousness. This assimilation of class and gender replaced the openness of Mao's early view in which he had called on women to seek individual freedom and equality and to oppose any authoritarian domination and spiritual shackling. Next, I will make three critiques on Mao's late view of women's equality: first, there was not really equal pay for equal work; second, class reduction theory was not a solution to women's equality; and third, Mao's authoritarianism suppressed women's independent seeking of equality. Thus, inequality persisted under Mao's call of substantive equality for Chinese women.

First, Mao's late view on women has two main features: advocating women's participation in production and in politics. These two are very important and absolutely necessary, but not sufficient without other considerations. The problems in the practice of equal pay for equal work—and the small proportion (almost 10 percent) of female cadres at different leading levels—tell the truth that the inequity of social arrangements converged with the spiritual shackles of old ideologies to prevent women from competing fairly with men in production and in political life. Thus, ending women's lower economic position required not only that they participate in production and political activities, but also that fair conditions of competition existed between the genders.

Mao pointed out the disadvantageous situation of working women in his investigation at Xun Wu in 1930: In addition to the responsibilities of domestic work and field labor, rearing children is the specific duty of women; therefore, women's work is much harder and far more demanding than that of men. However, Mao's late view and policy on women's equality did not deeply explore women's double burden. Instead, Mao simply assumed "Women can hold up half the sky," but women's sky would be twice as much as men's. How could Chinese women reach up to those double-standard demands and be equal to men in a substantive way? The policy of equal pay for equal work is not really equality to women in their reality of double-burdened situations. Nevertheless, Mao did not undertake deeper investigations into why gender inequality endured, but stressed instead that the abolition of class society is the basic condition for realizing equality, and this view reflected Engels's position:

> The situation of disrespect for women's rights did not appear until the classed society began . . . Only at the time when there are no classes in the society, when all hard labor becomes easy with the help of machines, and agriculture is mechanized, will real equality between men and women finally be achieved. (ACWF 1988, 61)

According to Mao's prediction, it will require a long historical transformation to achieve women's emancipation, but is it true that class annihilation is the only requirement for women's emancipation? It is clear that Mao says that mechanization, as well as the abolition of class society, is necessary for women's liberation, but this suggests that physical weakness, as well as property relations, are factors in women's subordination. He also said in his talk to Andre Malraux in 1958: "To liberate women is not to manufacture washing machines."[16] At this point, Mao still asserted that the most important factor in liberating women was not to change their material situation but to change people's minds. So there was some inconsistency in Mao's views, related to his ambiguity about women's subordination. Mao was not mistaken in his assumption that women's liberation would be realized with class liberation through great social changes, but class liberation and class struggle cannot replace direct attention to women's liberation and their own efforts for gender equity.

Second, Mao's inconsistency in his view of liberating women is mainly due to his ambiguity about women's subordination and his class reduction of gender oppression. Recall that in his early view of women Mao pointed out two roots of women's oppression. One is men's immorality to women's reproductive disadvantage; the other is women's economic dependence on men. After the 1950s, Mao came to subsume gender oppression into class analysis and use a substantive model of equality in production to solve the problems of women's subordination.

Heidi Hartmann criticizes Marxist feminism in her lead article, "The Unhappy Marriage of Marxism and Feminism."[17] According to Hartmann, Marxists see class as the correct framework within which to understand women's position. Since women should be seen as part of the working class, the class struggle against capitalism should take precedence over any conflict between men and women. Sex conflict must not be allowed to interfere with class solidarity (Hartmann 1981, 31). During the Cultural Revolution in China, sex conflict was not allowed to advance for discussion because of the fear of class solidarity.

Hartmann raises two strategic considerations to improve the union of Marxism and feminism. She claims that a struggle to establish socialism must be a struggle in which groups with different interests form an alliance. So women should not trust men to liberate them after the revolution against capitalism, because there is no reason to think men would know better than women how to do that, and also there is no necessity for men to do so. In order to oppose women's continued oppression, women must have their own organizations and power base. The second strategy concerns the sexual division of labor. The practice of this division within capitalism gives women a sense of understanding what interdependence and needs are. Unlike women's position, men's position prevents many of them from recognizing both human needs for nurturance, sharing, etc., and the potential for meeting those needs in a nonhierarchical, non-patriarchal society. So women must raise men's consciousness by motivating them to move toward social transitions to a nonsexist society (Hartmann 1981, 32-33). These views encounter different responses and criticism.

In socialist China during Mao's time, it was impossible for women to employ the above two strategies, because only one dominant voice could be heard, and Mao did not allow any independent women's organizations. There was no mention of any inquiry into gender consciousness, but a top-down policy of equal pay for equal work.

My last critique concerns Mao's authoritarianism and his suppression of independent women's pursuit of equality. In *The Party's Resolutions about Some Historical Issues,*[18] Mao's "subjectivism" and his "style of arbitrary decision making" were mentioned as reasons that led him into the great mistakes of enlarging class struggle and launching the Proletarian Cultural Revolution.[19] However, one must ask, what is the root of his "subjectivism" and "arbitrary decision making"? How could these grave mistakes be supported and allowed to pervade the whole party, the whole country, and the whole people without any resistance? Two reasons were given in the *Resolutions*: the short history of the socialist movements compared with the long history of feudal influence, and the people's inability to eliminate all remnants of feudalism in a short period. In my view, these two are only the external factors that encouraged the common view of women's inferiority. The internal factor was obstinate dogmatism and monological essentialist thinking. The root of Mao's subjective mistakes resides within this essentialist pattern of thinking.

Elizabeth V. Spelman's book *Inessential Women* (1988) is well known as a representative work against gender essentialism in the feminist theoretical field.

As Spelman points out, essentialists retain two key points: the universalization of their claims, and the authority of dominating theorists. Hence, they fall into false generalization and exclude other voices or differences.

I agree with the two charges against universal feminism in Spelman's argument: false generalization and the exclusion of other's voices. Theorists cannot universalize ideas from their own position and so are likely to concentrate on issues affecting their own group but not others. When this occurs, feminist theories face the danger of making unfounded assumptions of shared gender oppression and shared suffering from sexism. But here the question arises: Does anti-essentialism lead to the self-defeat of feminism? Is there any way for feminist theorists to address their common interests and aims among the different situations of different women? In other words, we may ask, if we take feminism seriously, as we already do, then what kind of generalization about women's issues would be the best and who will be the best candidates to theorize women's experiences?

As Spelman points out, given the heterogeneity of women and women's situations, it may seem as if it is impossible to make any well-founded yet nontrivial statements about *all* women. But, it "doesn't automatically follow that no generalizations about women are possible" (1988, 183). What Spelman wants to say is that if there is any truth about all women, it cannot be based on a single situation of any group of women. So she suggests that we keep our theories as a conjunction of different voices as they are. All feminists are equally apprentices, and we do not need any master to be an arbiter and determine controversies among us. Allowing differences to co-exist seems to be the safest way to keep away from the accusation of "imperialism" (185).

Remember that both Engels and Mao observe that gender bias has no uniformity among different classes. Working women's situation is supposedly much better than that of rich women in their concrete sexual oppression. In the feudal society of China, landlord-class women perhaps had a more miserable history than peasant women because the rich women's environment was full of Confucian tastes. Sexual oppression is not symmetrical with other forms of oppression, and they may be contrary to each other in some cases. The intersection among different oppressions also reminds us that any single focus on one oppression is not adequate to analyze women's issues. Since different women face different problems in their particular situations, feminist theorists should work out better theories that can explain the complicated connections between gender oppression and other oppressions. In order to do that, the more voices included, the more correction, the more original thoughts will gain. Anti-essentialism as a serious self-criticism would not lead to the self-defeat of feminism, but rather to a hope for a new development of a type of good social theories which will be more inclusive rather than exclusive, open rather than dogmatic.

In his later years Mao believed that only he could represent the best interests of all Chinese, including women, but he lacked concrete analysis of differences of gender in the situations of women and men. Hence, Mao held an "essentialist" class view of humanity as a whole, and therefore was gender blind in his policy of sameness of women and men. Thus, his substantive model of women's equality in production plus his dominant centralization of the many complex issues of women served to mute and puzzle women and to fill their already overburdened lives with unhappiness.

In conclusion, both Mao's early and late views of women show that he already realized that women could be regarded as a distinct group and as the most oppressed group. Nevertheless he remained ambiguous about the distinctions between women's liberation and class liberation; he did not investigate the relationship between these two, for he held class as the essence and used class analysis as the only universalized applicable weapon. Although Mao admitted that women's oppression had different characteristics from class oppression, he never allowed an analysis that put class oppression second. Hence, Mao's view of class prevented all possibilities of investigating the relation between women's liberation and class liberation. From the above overview, I find that the basic weakness of Mao's view of women is his essentialist, authoritarian method that excludes those who hold other views that may be valuable in clarifying women's issues, including women's equality.

Notes

1. See the documents of the Third Plenary of the Eleventh Central Committee of the CCP, which pointed out Mao's mistake of expanding class struggle and made a turning point of the party's focus on economic development. Also see Xu Quan-xing 1995, 501.

2. Kang Keqing (1912-): Married the commander of the Communist forces, Zhu De (1886-1976), at the Communist base on Jinggangshan in 1930, and since then involved herself with women's work. She served as director of the political department of the eighth Route Army from 1937 to 1945; was elected a member of the standing committee of the Democratic Women's Federation from 1949 to 1957, and was secretary in 1957; was elected chair of the Women's Federation in 1978 and reelected from 1983 to 1988 and was honorary chair after 1988. See Wolfgang Bartke 1991, 258-59.

3. Kang Keqing, "Chairman Mao Leads Us to the Road of Complete Emancipation of Women," in *People's Daily*, September 22, 1977.

4. Soviet areas refer to Communist bases, developed from Yenan to other places. The city of Yenan served as the general headquarters of the CCP from 1936 to 1947. See Dorothy Perkins 1999, 594.

5. See Kang Keqing, "Chairman Mao Leads Us to the Road of Complete Emancipation of Women," in *People's Daily*, September 22, 1977.

6. All China Women's Federation (ACWF), *Mao Zedong, Zhou Enlai, Liu Shaoqi, and Zhu De On Women's Liberation* (Beijing: People's Press, 1988), 45.

7. Hunan Women Federation, *Funuxuegailun* (*Introduction to Women Studies*), (Changsha: Hunan Press, 1987), 154.

8. Shaanxi Province Women's Federation, *Statistics on Chinese Women* (*1949-1989*) (Beijing: China Statistical Publishing, 1990), 572.

9. *Honqi* (*Red Flag*): the official magazine of the CCP.

10. All China Women's Federation (ACWF), *Important Documents of Chinese Women's Movement* (Beijing: People's Press, 1979), 135-36.

11. See Zhang, "Build up the Country Economically, Manage the Household Thriftily, and Strive for Socialist Construction," in *People's Daily*, July 3, 1973.

12. See Liu Chao, "Safeguarding Women's Interests," in *Peking Review*, March, 1974.

13. See Bob Avakian (1979), chapter 6.

14. See Xu Quan-xing (1995), chapter 4, section 1.

15. "Let All Women Rise Up," in *People's Daily*, March 8, 1974.

16. See Marilyn B. Young, ed., *Women in China: Studies in Social Change and Feminism* (Ann Arbor: University of Michigan, Center for Chinese Studies, 1973), next to copyright page.

17. Heidi Hartmann, "The Unhappy Marriage of Marxism and Feminism," in *Women and Revolution: A Discussion of the Unhappy Marriage of Marxism and Feminism*, ed. Lydia Sargent (Montreal: Black Rose Books, 1981), 1-41.

18. *The Party's Resolutions about Some Historical Issues*, passed at the Sixth Plenary of the Eleventh Central Committee of the CCP on June 27, 1981.

19. See *Important Documents of the CCP since the Third Plenary of the Eleventh Central Committee of the CCP*, 155.

Chapter Four

Equal Opportunity in the Post-Mao Period

After Mao died in 1976, the Chinese Communist Party dramatically changed the focus of its work from class struggle to economic construction: first, the party reflected on its history since the founding of the New China and the correction of Mao's class reductionism by issuing a packet of documents of the Eleventh Central Committee; second, the party created the market policy to speed economic growth and significantly improve the material life of the Chinese people; and third, an open-door foreign policy to the West was implemented in all fields. Nevertheless, the transformation period has so far remained a kind of "dark age" for women's political representation (Wang 1999, 19). A popular male sociologist argued for women's difference from men and against women's employment during the shortage of jobs (Zheng 1995, chapter 9). The deteriorating situation for women was rationalized by this view. The need for stability and peace for the whole nation coincided with the rehabilitation of Confucianism, which advocates women's traditional roles, family values, and loyalty to the state. However, no one has overtly challenged the idea of sex equality. Instead, a new interpretation favors the idea of equal opportunity.

In this chapter, I will discuss this new version of equality for women, examine various views on the changes of women's status in the economic transitional period, and assess the impact of these social changes on women's equality. I will discuss Zheng's view of women's difference and identity and argue that Chinese women still need the social ideal of equality to combat unequal treatment in the midst of economic changes. Finally, I will reflect on current discussions about family values, domestic violence, and marital rape, and I will argue that Western feminist challenges to family values, sex differences, and sex roles help Chinese women realize that their own interests and needs should be an equal concern in the pursuit of equality. Chinese feminist thinking should include the political goal of ending women's subordination by presenting multidimensional challenges to the existing norms, and these challenges cannot occur without a democratic environment.

Various Views on Changes in Women's Status and Equality

This section will explain the impact on Chinese women of wide-ranging social, political, and economic transformations and an opening-up to the outside world. The retreat of the state and the advance of the market have allowed free discussion of the changes in women's situations: women's studies and other autonomous activities have begun to grow and flourish. Some scholars describe it: "The flow of information and traveling of ideas, free thinking, communicating, and even organizing became feasible" (Lin, Liu, and Jin 2000, 109). I will focus on three aspects of their scholarly investigations: how the changes in the political, economic, and psychological arena have influenced women's equality.

Political Impact

Scholar Wang Qi investigated "State-Society Relations and Women's Political Participation."[1] According to Wang, on the surface, the transition period has so far remained a kind of "dark age" for women's political representation. This seems true if you look at the sharply declining proportion of women cadres[2] at the basic-level: In the 1950s, 70 percent of the villages in rural China had at least one female head or director, while in the 1990s only 10 percent of villages throughout the country had a female head. In 1993, women accounted for only about 3.8 percent of county township administrators, 5.9 percent of county heads, and 5.8 percent of municipal managers (19). These sharply declining proportions definitely generate "challenges to the established Communist ideology of gender equality and its public consensus" (Lin, Liu, and Jin 2000, 108).

Why has the transition from communism in post-Mao China turned out to be so disadvantageous for women with regard to their political representation? Wang argues that women's political participation in Mao's time was not an autonomous action but a given political policy from above, which would be drawn back when the party made a retreat and reformed its general line in multidimensional aspects. The argument goes as follows: Strong state input facilitated the inroad of women into China's local leadership structure; also the party's dominant policies decided women's participation in political leadership. This input and these policies made women politically dependent on the state for support and legitimacy. As a result, the political transition of the post-Mao period, marked by the retreat of the state from society, has undermined the foundations of women's political participation. Now, women are entering a new historical phase of development that advocates self-reliant competition for their political participation without the support of the state. In such gender-blind competition, women are vulnerable in joining the political arena (Wang 1999, 20).

Wang notices that in order to spur economic development, the reform leadership has discarded Maoist egalitarian ideology in favor of a kind of economic liberalism based on the principle of equal opportunity. The reconceptualization of socialism in economic terms and the recognition of geographic and social inequality as an inevitable phenomenon of socialist development at the current primary stage worked together with the mechanism of the market economy, "leading to the rise of a competitive mentality and the rejection of gender equality as a fundamental principle" (1999, 31). Under this principle, the standards for selecting cadres as reform leaders must discard the Maoist emphasis on political loyalty and revolutionary consciousness. The new cadre formula places great importance on "ability" and thereby fosters a kind of merit worship in China. Given women's general position (less educated than men and so on), these new cadre criteria have worked to women's disadvantages. According to the census of 1982, women account for nearly 80 percent of the country's illiterates and semi-illiterates, and 77 percent of the female working population is engaged in agriculture, and "women also lag behind men in terms of tangible work results because women cadres have been mostly assigned to woman-work or family planning, work that does not provide immediately tangible outcomes" (31).

Disregarding these gender-different situations, a male professor argues for a gender-blind view of equal competition and the requirement that candidates be measured by ability only in order to win leadership: "One must participate in politics and government on the basis of what one is capable of, no matter whether one is male or female" (Xiang 1993, 93). Wang objects that this seemingly gender-neutral argument actually has tended to promote anti-female behavior in the alteration of China's ideological course and the cadre criteria (Wang 1999, 32). Wang does not say in her article why these criteria are not neutral, but anti-female. I will suggest one reason why this argument might be anti-female. If one's capabilities depend on one's education and background, then if women as a group have been excluded from education, training, etc., they would not have the proper capabilities because of the previous discrimination against them. Traditional ideology such as Confucian views on women also should be held responsible for women's lack of education; the Confucian belief that "Being untalented is a virtue in women" would encourage parents to invest in their girl's education last. The social norms of women's subordinated roles in the family also contribute to preventing women from continuing professional training and education.

There are other perspectives to explain the decline in women's political participation: Li Xiaojiang pointed out (1988) that women have not themselves struggled for equality but have received it from above during their assimilation into the world of men. As Wang described, "Li Xiaojiang defines women's political participation not quantitatively but qualitatively," and Li puts forward a qualitative standard for measuring whether or not women have "true participation in politics" (Wang 1999, 37). According to this measure, what matters in women's political involvement are two aspects of consciousness: their self-

awareness as women and their collective consciousness as members of the female sex. Without these two aspects of consciousness, Li claims that any other
form of participation would be false and symbolic (Li 1989, 33).

When women's "subjective" and "group" consciousness are taken as the
criteria of participation, the level of women's participation gained in state-
imposed political equality through the quota system should not be taken as a true
indication of women's political influence. In this view, women's lower percentage in leadership now is not an indication of political retreat. Thus, Wang claims
that "as long as women's voices are heard it is not so important to be a cadre"
(1999, 38).

In my view, Wang is right to emphasize the importance of the two specifically female consciousnesses raised by Li and also to stress women's ability to
perceive their situations. I appreciate her point that what matters in political representation is the expression of women's independent voices rather than that of
the cadre's official voice. I would further explore the issue of women's quota as
follows.

First, many feminists, especially Western feminists, argue that women have
better insight into women's needs. There should be quotas for women in governing positions to better represent women's perspectives and their real needs.
Hence, the current retreat of women's quotas in the official operating of the state
will harm women in ways which will decrease women's voices or prevent their
voices from being heard.

Nevertheless, there are concerns about who will express women's authentic
voice. As we saw in chapter 3, women are not essential, as Spelman (1988)
pointed out, and women are different in their social status. The women selected
for office would be the privileged, and they might not represent less privileged
women. Furthermore, some women could be controlled by men and do nothing
to promote women's equality or just be tools of the party line like the women's
federations in Mao's time. What would make women's representation matter in
political participation?

I would emphasize that both types of participation—being a cadre of the
state or independent women scholars—are very important for allowing women's
voices to be heard. Women as a less privileged group do need state support for
their self-improvement in their current situation. It is not women's fault that they
are unable to perform equally with men in the economic transition: it is the result of cultural and political norms; hence, women deserve the state's special
concern and support. We need at least two steps for women's participation in
political leadership. First is the necessary step: if women do not participate politically, they have no chance to express women's voices. Without a certain
number of female cadres at the top decision-making level, there would be no
concern for women's special needs and interests and the enforcement of those
needs. The greater the participation, the better representation women can have.
Some Western feminists argue that in order to challenge men, women's percent-

age should be over 30. Through participation and learning, women would know how the political process and institutions work and how women as a group are treated under those political agendas. The next step is preparing women with the two types of consciousness for their political participation. Women cadres should be made aware of both self-consciousness as a woman and collective consciousness as members of the female sex. Through these two efforts, Chinese women will be able to pursue their equality in various social arenas. Nevertheless, the radical decline of women's participation in the political arena during the transformation period shows that women's needs and interests are more likely to be neglected in male-dominated decision making.

Economic Impact

The economic transition has brought about radical changes in women's lives. Women were the first to be laid off and became a target for unemployment in urban areas and in rural districts. "The feminization of agriculture" is one of the many outcomes of the radical changes happening in China now (Zhang Xiaoquan 1999, 60-63; Tan 1995, 163; Gao 1994). Through a discussion of Xiaoquan H. Zhang's view in her "Understanding Changes in Women's Status in the Context of the Recent Rural Reform,"[3] I will examine the causes of feminization of agriculture and its implications for women's equality.

Zhang did a case study in the northern Chinese village of Dongdatun in the summer of 1994, and her view of women's status in the transition era was based on interviews that included various women's perspectives. According to her observation, "women enjoy more freedom and flexibility" as a result of the economic changes, and many hold a positive view of the reform programs. Increased opportunities to earn money through domestic or outside labor (sideline production at home or working in town-and-village enterprises) were available for women. These changes made women "more independent, more courageous in terms of resisting parental or patriarchal control over their lives, and more confident about fulfilling their aspirations through their own efforts" (Zhang Xiaoquan 1999, 55-56).

In the process of rural labor transfer, more women than men have remained in the agricultural sector. Many women, particularly those in the poor northwestern region, have been kept at low-level, unskilled farm work, while men have left the land in search of better opportunities and jobs in the cities. The proportion of women engaged in agricultural work has grown since the transformation, whereas that of men has declined. One case study in a village in central China in 1989 revealed that 71 percent of women compared with only 21 percent of men were engaged in full-time agricultural work, indicating much less occupational mobility and diversity among women than men (Zhang Xiaoquan 1999, 61).

These facts reveal women's disadvantaged position in the transfer of rural labor from agricultural to nonagricultural and industrial occupations, as Zhang states. What are the causes of women's disadvantage? According to her analysis, the principal causes as stressed by the official press are the so-called "low quality" of the female labor force as a result of poor literacy, and less occupational training. But lower skill levels may not be real reasons at all. She prefers a woman's perspective: "the existing unfair familial and social arrangements that endow men with greater freedom and mobility are mainly responsible." Here, Zhang means that most women need to stay at home and maintain local residency to take care of children and older family generations. But men are supposed to search for better jobs and opportunities to earn more in order to support the family. This does not explain the situation of those young women who have not gotten married. Nevertheless, girls are always the last to receive their family's investment in education. Therefore girls are less competitive in the job market. Also, traditional cultural values that regard men as superior to women and value men over women "have ensured that men and male children receive preferential treatment in education and training." Thus, it is not difficult to see that "the official attribution of rural women's disadvantaged position in an increasingly competitive labor market . . . to the so-called "low quality" of women has created a *de facto* effect of blaming the victims of sexual prejudice themselves for the social disadvantages they have experienced" (Zhang Xiaoquan 1999, 62-63). It also obscures the real reasons for women's low positions in the economic transition. Zhang's insightful analysis helps us see the dialectical relationship between causes and consequences: the so-called "low quality" of the female labor force may not be the cause of women's disadvantages but instead the consequence of unfair social arrangements accompanied by the traditional values that place men over women.

Next I will address the state of rural women in the labor market. One of the substantial outcomes of the economic transformation in China was the establishment of the labor market, and rural women became active participants in vying for job opportunities. Nevertheless, as Huang Xiyi states, "No matter which part women play in the newly established labor market, they encounter a range of disadvantages in terms of jobs, pay, and working conditions."[4] Song Lina supports this view by analyzing "the subordinate position of women in migration."[5] Huang adds an important point to other research about the elements that have shaped gender inequality during the economic transition. She mentions that local authorities frequently check registration cards of migrant women workers, which allows employers to treat them differently from local women. So in spite of official service to improve the women's situation, many government officials actually pushed migrant women to the bottom.

There have been a large number of rural migrants rushing to the cities in search of jobs since the mid-1980s. Migration in China involves more physical insecurity and hardship, but it also means hope of getting a job and personal development. Do rural women have a good chance of getting urban jobs? What are the elements that affect their migratory behavior? What is the state's attitude and how does it affect women's migration?

Generally, the labor market operates under the principles of the social division of labor and social hierarchies. In a hierarchical labor market, women's employment faces structural restrictions. Huang calls this vertical segregation, dividing men and women along differences in pay, skills, status, and promotion prospects. According to Huang, many social scholars have investigated these segregations and differences, and one approach is especially worth noting: "the Marxist approach argues that women have been drawn into unskilled, low-paid jobs to aid capital accumulation because employers can maximize their profits by hiring female labor at the lowest wage (Beechey, 1986). Therefore the labor process from the beginning of industrial development is both 'capitalist' and 'genderist' (Bladley, 1989)" (Huang Xiyi 1999, 90). Huang realizes that this approach focuses on the demand side of the labor market, but it may lack analysis from the supply side. Both kinds of analysis, according to Huang, should consider political influence on gender differentiation in labor markets. She points out that "the influence of the state is another important element in shaping gender inequality" (92) According to Huang, although other authors such as Elisabeth Croll (1985), Delia Davin (1988), and Shirin Rai (1992) have acknowledged the significance of the state's impact on women's economic activity, they fail to theorize adequately the process of marketization. Huang attempts to remedy some of those gaps in the research on gender in the labor market by analyzing the relationship between women and the state, in particular, how officials treat rural women migrants.

Domestic service is a main source of employment for migrant women and is dominated by them. "Traditionally in China, serving others confers less dignity, brings less reward and does not require as much education and training" (Huang Xiyi 1999, 95). No urban women, especially young women, are willing to work as domestic servants even if they are unemployed, since those services are not only low paid and boring but are looked down upon as the lowest social status. However, the local women have more means to appeal for better jobs or try for new opportunities compared to those immigrant women from the poor, rural areas. Here we see a difference between women as urban residents and women of migration. Those women migrants (most of them young and single) occupy a position at the lowest rung in the hierarchy of the labor market. In the rural/urban division of labor, rural women are often assigned to physical work such as waiting tables and cleaning, while the local urban women are employed as accountants and shop assistants. Furthermore, women migrants encounter suffering from marriage: they are compelled to leave their jobs when they marry, "while married local women are allowed to stay until they become pregnant" (99). One reason for the discrimination against married women migrants is the cost of housing and nursing facilities. (The state policies require employers to pay for nursing facilities because the state is implementing the one-child family plan.) But local women as insiders of the community may have less cost in their marriage. According to Huang, migrant rural women encounter two types of discriminatory treatment: they are treated differently from local women and differently from migrant men. Huang also points out that the hierarchical division of migrant and local female workers is reinforced by state policies. Local authorities frequently check the registration cards of migrant laborers, making the situation of rural women in temporary jobs worse. In effect, this "allows employers to treat migrant workers badly and to fail to fulfill their agreements" (100).

Huang highlights not only the differences between men and women, and between employers and employees, but also the differentiation between local female and migrant female workers. She claims that the attitude of the state and employers toward migrants is the main reason why female migrants choose to complain little or not to speak out in the face of discrimination, because any attempt to sue or complain often has a negative repercussion on their jobs. "For the same reason, rural women in the more advanced rural areas choose to work locally, as I discovered during my fieldwork in Cangnan" (Huang Xiyi 1999, 100). Here Huang argues that the interrelationship between political factors and cultural elements rather than merely economic concerns (seeking to maximize profits by hiring the cheapest female labor) determines how migrant female workers are treated when they get married.

According to this argument, it is pointless for a migrant woman to struggle to keep her factory job, as she will eventually lose it anyway when she marries. The unstable situation of migrant employment makes contractual land in the countryside especially important. With the introduction of the household responsibility system in agriculture by the state at the beginning of the economic transformation period, peasants obtained the right to a piece of farmland for a period of fifteen to thirty years. The entrance of a bride into a rural household will bring an additional quota of land to the groom's household. A newly married migrant couple have to give top priority to family interests in the groom's village, which will be their permanent home. This explanation of why marriage is a turning point for female migrants helps explain the feminization of agriculture. "Unlike men, women are also expected to fulfill their responsibilities for housework and childcare when doing farm work" (Huang Xiyi 1999, 101). The state and acceptable norms, social expectations, and arrangements force women to choose to remain on their land. The state and culture remain a powerful force during the formation of the new social structure in that they maintain social and economic order during the transformation. The significance of Huang's research is to recognize this complicated combination of the political, cultural, and marketing facts. "Rural women have contributed most to capital accumulation" (105), but their social position is the lowest.

Although these women make large contributions to economic development, their contributions are not rewarded and needs are unmet. In Mao's time, top-down policies were supposed to protect women's interests in a patriarchal society. Now, the party's political retreat laid down the burden of improving the status on women, while the state's intervention in the market made migrant women's status worse. Those women seem to choose to keep silent for the good of their family, but their "choices" sound like the only ones they could have made in the context of familial and social pressures and their limited choices, which in return further the stereotyped view of women's subordination.

Psychological and Life-View Impact

Women's subordinated situations made a once-popular slogan less plausible. Abandoning the idea that "women can do everything men can," more and more women have adopted the Confucian traditional view of women's roles of following men. He Qinglian worries about women's orientation of their life value and realizes the seriousness of women losing their social position. In her analysis, women have encountered too many pressures in the economic transformation, including difficulty in finding jobs, sexual risks in the workplace, marriage breakups, and, particularly, women's retreat to the traditional customs of following men. These social pressures have forced women back to believing in the so-called women's virtues in the household and to putting their hope in a good marriage rather than in self-development. Women have changed their self-image during their experiences. Women have begun to redesign their self-image according to male demand: being soft, beautiful, and compliant have become women's standards since traditional Chinese men like women with these characteristics. "Strong women" have become out of date, and they have been blamed for not appreciating or being appropriate in family life, and young, pretty women are praised as replacements for successful men's ex-wives (He 2001, 77-78).

He Qinglian describes several social pressures on women including unemployment, sexual harassment, and family breakups[6], and women's attitudes toward marriage and life values. First, some enterprises avoid hiring female candidates by raising female entrance scores on employment tests; e.g., male candidates would need a score of 260, while females must earn 320 to meet the entrance standard. Some foreign corporations use female workers only during their so-called golden age, from sixteen to twenty years old, in order to avoid pregnancy and breast-feeding. Second, female workers are the first to be laid off by employers, and they are less likely to return to the job compared with men. Third, female workers tend to work a long time under bad conditions: many factories lack necessary safety protections and women are poisoned by dust, noise, and high temperatures. In one instance, seventy thousand female workers were poisoned by benzene in a shoe factory in Fujian, as reported in *China Women Daily* (Jan. 15-17, 1996). Fourth, female employees, especially those in offices, are easy targets of sexual harassment; they are unlikely to sue their bosses out of concern for their jobs. Yet another pressure on women, according to He, is changes in marriage: successful men want young and pretty females to replace their ex-wives, and many men in high positions have concubines (so-called Bao Er Nai phenomena, keeping a second wife) (He, 79-83).

These social pressures make women feel insecure and less independent, and many women believe "a good marriage is much better than doing the best in hard work" (He, 82). But this may not be true considering women's vulnerability within their marriages. As He describes, women must simultaneously meet men's needs for a virtuous wife and lusty concubine in order to prevent divorce. The pressures from marriage are the most serious stress in women's lives, and they affect women's psychology in developing their life values. From the 1980s the divorce rate in China has nearly tripled, and the highest rate of divorce is among people of middle age and older. In He's analysis, the economic status of these generations was the most improved, but this has influenced a new model of marriage in the 1990s. In the middle of the 1990s, the husband's age was typically ten years more than his wife's, an increase in age difference of 14.5 percent compared with the same situation in 1987. This reflects the phenomenon of a new group of rich men who divorce their wives and marry young and pretty women in new developing districts in southern coast areas. Some men claim that a man needs to marry three times, at age thirty, forty, and fifty, to have a perfect life. In other words, their perfect mate is a woman in "the golden age," or a concubine. On the other side, more and more women experience the so-called three episodes of a virtuous woman's life: self-sacrifice and caring for the family when young; helping and satisfying a husband's need for young lovers when in middle age; being abandoned or keeping silent when getting old. We see the difference of genders in the changes of marriage during the economic transformation. The social norm of women's sacrifice for the sake of family most likely benefits the husband, but does not help women raise their self-consciousness. It makes the situation of women even worse, because the male's idea of perfection is a trap for women that is mistaken as natural, fashionable, and worthy of seeking. According to He (82-88), this kind of trap has harmed vulnerable women the most, and it is a serious social problem that may influence the "quality" of the Chinese people and the "prospect" of the nation. By the "quality" of people, she means their ability to analyze what is right and what is wrong in their moral practice of romantic relationship and sexuality; and by the "prospect" she means the hope and dignity of China in the future.

Women's general situation in China today appears much as He summarized it, although her summary may reflect only the dark side of women's situation. Other scholars have a somewhat different take on those unpleasant pictures of women's lives and women's responses to their reality. Wang Xingjuan[7] describes two breakthroughs of women's self-consciousness (Wang Xingjuan 1995b). The first one is the waking of women's liberation from the feudal shackles under Mao's call of "women hold up half of the sky." Women got the legal right to be equal to men and started to realize gender identity, being proud of what women can do in production but puzzled by the problems in their lives. The second breakthrough is a kind of self-consciousness as a person without dependence on the state during the economic reform. The competition encourages women to be self-reliant and helps women realize how to develop their own potential as a complete person rather than as dependent on a husband. But how can women invest their selves in both categories—public and family domains—and also be self-fulfilled? Wang did not go into details to reply to this question, and she claimed the second breakthrough would be much more difficult than the state program of gender equality, and it must go deep into the shaping of personal identity, which calls for fundamental challenges in many ways (1995b, 197-98). It seems that family values alone cannot solve women's problems because these problems relate to the whole social structure. Women and all Chinese people need to raise their gender consciousness and be aware of gender relations in power. Wang's view is a brief outline that is very insightful in encouraging women to strive for a better position in the new period of the economic transformation. I would add that in the second breakthrough, women especially need the social ideal of gender equality, because women's actual inequality is not the cause but the consequence of the unequal treatment and devaluation of women by society. I will move on to the specific argument about this issue next.

On Zheng's Argument of Equal Opportunity

The most influential and popular view on the inequality of social arrangements between the sexes appeared at the time of great changes in women's status in the economic transition and was written by a rising star sociologist, Zheng Yefu. In the book *On Prices: A New Perspective of Sociology* (1995), Zheng argues that under Mao the political equality of men and women was imposed that brought about an absurd "inequality": "the stronger are deprived by the weak." Hence, the equality of men and women led to similarity of sexes—a poor, colorless, and monotonous society (1995, 74). He states that under the current economic transition, the economic efficiency principle will not favor the policy of sex equality but equal opportunity regardless of sex. He simply assumes that women were favored with the official imposition of gender policy, and that strong men were deprived by the unfair dictum of "equal work for equal pay" in Mao's time. He suggests that women as the weaker sex should stay at home and support the stronger to go out for jobs. I will explain why his argument is invalid.

Before addressing the issue of equality of men and women, Zheng quotes
Fei Xiaotong to explain the differential mode of association in China. Fei says in
his essay *Xiangtu Zhongguo*,[8] first Chinese edition [1947]:

> Social relationships in China possess a self-centered quality. Like the
> ripples formed from a stone thrown into a lake, each circle spreading
> out from the center becomes more distant and at the same time more
> insignificant. With this pattern, we are faced with the basic character-
> istic of Chinese social structure, or what the Confucian school has
> called *renlun* (human relationships). What is *lun*? To me, insofar as it
> is used to describe Chinese social relationships, the term itself signi-
> fies the ripple-like effect created from circles of relationships that
> spread out from the self, an effect that produces a pattern of discrete
> circles . . . Lun stresses differentiation (1992, [1947] 65).

Fei's description of the Chinese *lun* is always used to support a society of
hierarchy and differences between people. Zheng also emphasizes differences
between the sexes to argue that the so-called "equality of men and women" in
Mao's time came at the price of upsetting the social order and the effectiveness
of the economy. His argument goes as follows: First, as he says, there seem to
be two kinds of inequality between men and women: either that men dominate
women or women dominate men. Why have men dominated women in the long
history of human civilization? According to Zheng, the answer is simple; men
are stronger and fit more into the intrinsic human pursuit of competition and
plunder. It is obvious that this assumes a biological explanation. He claims that
it is not the discovery of fatherhood that makes human society more competitive
than matriarchy, as Russell thought (1929, 26), but rather the innate human nature of competition favors men since they are stronger than women (Zheng
1995, 66). Since this intrinsic human nature, in his claim, would continue despite changes in modes of production, there is nothing wrong with the system of
patriarchy, because it is an inevitable pattern of association (67). In Zheng's
view, the only price of patriarchy is that some very talented women are subdued
by its rigid norms. Nevertheless, in Zheng's words, natural patriarchy is based
on the efficiency principle through the division of labor, and thus it sounds fair
to let weak women stay at home doing household work, and let strong men go
out to earn more money. In addition, society needs to have a sense of tolerance
for some talented women.

   According to Zheng, Mao's call for women's liberation and equality in production broke through the normal pattern of the division of labor, "helped the
weak to overcome the strong, destroying the normal division of labor in the family domain. It went so far to make the weak feel not weak, and the strong lose
self-confidence they deserve." Thus, Chinese socialism bestowed on women a
favor by making men feel less strong and womanish so they would share household work. The political movement of women's liberation pushed Chinese

women to lose their female identification, too, in Zheng's words: women sought to be like men and take men's standards as a symbol of equality, and further-more, men's characteristics and values became more popular than those of women. It is ironic that women sought their liberation and equality through changing their identity into that of men. Finally, women are confused by the idea of women's liberation and equality because they cannot compete with men, and society is disordered and monotonous as a price of the absurdity of equality (1995, 69-71). Inferring from the supposedly natural preference of strong men to dominate women in a patriarchal society, and the price of women's liberation and equality, Zheng concludes that tolerance of equal opportunity is acceptable, but that it is also necessary to keep the traditional cultural pattern of sexual iden-tity that implies the inequality of men and women. As Lin describes Zheng's suggestion from his price argument: "gender inequality should be restored in both theory and policies" (Lin 1995, 57). The "normal" division of labor be-tween the weak and the strong sex should be restored: the weak should go back to their "natural" place, unpaid domestic work, and the stronger should go to the free market to compete.

The new justification of gender inequality has been welcomed by other scholars, e.g., Sun Liping, who insists that resuming traditional gender roles and letting women return home would be the only way out of the now-mounting unemployment predicament (Lin 1995, 57). As we saw in the previous section, many women are indeed returning to domestic work and there is a trend toward feminization of agriculture. In the context of all the social, family, and psycho-logical pressures, women are forced to "choose" their subordinated roles, but those roles trap them in their oppression as women. Women should be aware of the real causes of their subordinated positions instead of believing that it is the consequence of their inherent inequality as Zheng argues. I will challenge Zheng's argument by asking the following questions: what is the difference be-tween the social ideal of sex equality in an abstract sense, and practical issues in applying this idea of equality? Why should we believe that men are naturally strong, more aggressive, and suitable for competition? How should we evaluate the traditional view of *lun* and the efficiency principle in economy? Have women been favored by the policy of "equal pay for equal work" and have stronger men been deprived? My analysis will lead to different conclusions from those of Zheng.

Question One: Although inequality between men and women has existed throughout history and is present in most nations of the world, the feminist fight for a social ideal of equality for women has continued unabated over the past one hundred years. As we see, there is a significant difference between the so-cial ideal of equality and the problematic issues involved in putting this ideal into practice. In addition, the long patriarchal tradition has considerable power to retain its political stability by continuing to justify male dominance. Hence every step of the feminist fight for women's equality has encountered tremendous difficulties and hardships in the concrete contexts of women's life experiences. Chinese feminists began fighting for the ideal of equality at the beginning of the twentieth century, and the ideal was favored by the state during Mao's time. As I showed in chapters 2 and 3, early Chinese feminism was problematic but these problems do not mean that the feminist pursuit of the ideal of equality is unrealistic or unworthy. The practical difficulties in this pursuit show people the difficulty and complexity of women's issues or human issues of equality, but should not discourage their work. Since the relationship between the ideal and its tremendous practical problems cannot be completely separated from Zheng's discussion of the issues of equality, his lack of concern for the ideal of equality has led him to an unconvincing argument. In fact, he replaces the ideal of equality with the notion of women's practical inequality in the period of economic changes, and encourages a policy of female unemployment to leave more room for male employment. Here he is unconcerned with the social ideal of equality for women while he tries to solve problems of unequal treatment of genders by a seemingly fair policy of economic efficiency. This simplifies the complicated issues of equality and his gender-blind view actually favors one sex. Also, we see political interference in economic competition by the official checking of migrants' registration cards in the job markets, and sex differences in the official rules for retirement age (e.g., men's retirement age is fifty-two; women's is forty-five). Zheng assumes biological causes for gender inequalities that are better explained by social causes. Now I will turn to the question of the so-called sex difference and power inequality in the relations between women and men that Zheng totally neglects.

Question Two: Zheng favors the efficiency principle of economics, and on his interpretation it advocates that the weak should engage in domestic work and the strong should participate in the market. First, the assumption that one sex is inherently stronger than the other has been challenged in many social investigations, especially in Western feminism. I do not support his assumption of women as the weaker sex but for now we can just consider the assumption problematic. The difference between weak and strong is based on old beliefs that come from the Chinese traditional view of women and men, as does Fei's idea of *lun*: it stresses differentiation and its ten relationships, including husbands and wives, the superiors and the inferiors, and it means "everyone should stay in his place" (Fei 1992, 65) to satisfy proper arrangements, classification, and social order. These old ideas of hierarchy in human relations easily lead to special advantages for special groups of people such as the idea that it is virtuous for women to follow men, which led to the cruel oppression of women in Chinese feudal society.

I am not denying that there are classifications and stratifications in human relationships, but it is not correct to expand these differences into the moral domain: to prescribe women's special virtues as being subordinate to men and to devalue women as less worthy of moral consideration. By contrast, the ideal of gender equality respects both men and women and every human being no matter how different everyone is. We should not intentionally encourage the difference between sexes or use the differences as excuses for favoring the dominant sex. In Zheng's argument of economic efficiency, without challenging the traditional favoritism granted to "strong men," he actually uses this traditional value to support his assumption that women are weak.

Even if women were weak, we should not enlarge the gap between the weak and the strong for the consideration of economic tyranny by the head of household. Zheng has not mentioned any consideration of domestic tyranny, family abuse, and women's unpaid work, but those considerations have been closely related to issues of sexual inequality. Also, even if men are stronger, that does not mean men should be in positions of power more than women. In addition, we all know most market jobs do not require physical strength but other abilities. Therefore, the argument that women should leave the job market for the sake of economic efficiency fails to meet the moral and political justifications for women's status.

Question Three: Are women favored by the state support of equality and have they plundered men's interests? Zheng does not give any statistical support for his assumption of "depriving by weak over strong," and so has he imagined this "absurd inequality"? The answer is evident in other scholars' investigations into "equal pay for equal work" in state policies of sex/gender equality. In the book *Revolution Postponed: Women in Contemporary China* (1985), Margery Wolf writes about the status of women workers in cities and in the countryside. She interviews one hundred women and ten men in a factory in Beijing and she quotes one woman: "Rush in the morning, stand in line at noon, headache in the afternoon, angry in the evening" (57). None of the men she talks with allude to this. It is interesting that when asked if they would rather have the life of a man or woman, none of the men interviewed wants to be a woman. If Zheng is correct in saying that women, as the weaker sex, get preferential treatment from state policy (equal pay for equal work) in order to earn the same as men, why do these men not want to obtain such favors by having the life of a woman?

One reason is that they know women have many "other" duties, such as cooking, cleaning, laundry, and child care, that must be squeezed into the hours before and after work and these duties are not paid. Wolf states:

> Although equal pay for equal work is a rule frequently cited, it is readily apparent that equal work is a myth among the older women in my sample. Their husbands are employed in industry and other state enterprises, whereas they are, by and large, in neighborhood workshops. Income figures I obtained for 236 women and men in Beijing and Shaoxing show that, on the average, the women are paid 71.7 percent of what men are paid—545.84 Chinese yuan per year for women and 761.01 per year for men. (Wolf 1985, 64)

These statistical investigations match what I observed during the 1970s. I experienced peasant women's lives in a big village, and I understood the meaning of supposed equal pay for equal work: women were not given preferential treatment but were burdened by double shifts of domestic and farm work. Through the above assessment of the three questions, I conclude women under Mao were not favored but were burdened by double shifts; the unpaid domestic work actually prevented women from gaining equal footing to compete with men in paid jobs. Women's disadvantaged position contributed to women's inequality in practice.

The issue of whether women should return home and stay there appeared as a hot topic in *Beijing Daily, Guangming Daily, Chinese Women Daily* and other journals in the late 1980s (Tong 1995, 191-96; Li Xiaojiang 1997, 385-88). Different views reflect the dilemma of women's double roles and their puzzle of different expectations. Only a few women are capable of playing both roles well. For example, some female leaders in the state try extra hard to play the family role by being especially concerned and caring for their husbands in order to get their understanding and support (Wang Xingjuan 1995a, 50-51). In fact, many men support women's employment as long as women can play family roles and bring more money into the family. They expect "their wives should be working type plus housekeeping type" (Tong 1995, 237). And Tong calls this a "double roles expectation" that is not only challenging the conservative expectation of women (just be good wives and devoted mothers), but is also pushing a high standard of women's development: "the unity of double role playing" (240).

Both Zheng's argument for women's exclusion from paid employment and the unity of women's double role playing attempt to shape women's identities according to men's expectations and men's likes or dislikes. Whether women should stay home or do double work is made to depend on how women should contribute to family well-being and to the husband's success, rather than on a woman's development according to her potential. Zheng notices that this social norm of fixed sex roles is the price of patriarchy: its domineering culture and lack of flexibility would suppress women who have talents and potential (1995, 68), but he does not pay attention to why males have no such problems or a similar price to pay. He simply assumes that it is natural and necessary to keep these norms, and therefore the unequal social arrangements between the sexes will continue without challenge.

The puzzle of women's identity and double roles will remain unsolved until women are willing to examine the political relationships found in sex/gender issues, particularly issues of equality. Many women are aware that changes in social conditions may help women play their roles better. For example, Li Jingzhi (1995) points out three ways to relieve the conflicts between women's roles and their personal development: socialization of household chores in order to liberate women from those burdens; changing the pattern of the division of labor and the social norms of men dominating and women following, into norms where both women and men are responsible for family work; and scientific management of household work in order to reduce the burden of family care and chores. These rough outlines (226-30) are quite right, but they require huge work under each title. The most difficult one is changing the old norms and customs that still preoccupy people's minds and developing the issue of women's equality as a social ideal to strive for.

In Li's investigation, "72.8 percent of people thought 'the husband's success is the success of the wife, hence the wife should support the husband wholeheartedly' and 51.1 percent of people agreed that 'men should put the society first and women should put the family first'" (1995, 228). These opinions reflect the powerful influence of the traditional view of gender relations: "Respectable men and humble, oppressed women." Without a thorough challenge to the traditional views of gender relations and without a desire for women's self and collective consciousness-raising, as Li Xiaojing advocates, how can Chinese women be liberated from these spiritual shackles and psychological pressures? Furthermore, mere ideological recognition of women's oppression will not be enough to gain women's equality. As I noted in my criticism of Mao's late view of women in chapter 3, there is a lot more to explore in social structural inequalities.

Current Discussion of Family Values, Domestic Violence, and Marital Rape

Traditional ethical education in China always emphasized the value of family and the common good of community. It follows from these values that one should have similar loyalty to the state (the largest community) and love for the father of the state. Both traditional views like Confucianism and modern ideas such as Maoism advocate loyalty to the state, seen as inseparable from one's filial emotion to the family and one's loyalty to a marriage partner. Nevertheless, being loyal to an abusive husband is not morally right and cannot solve problems at all. Along with the great changes of economic development, many issues such as domestic violence and marital rape have been exposed and debated. How are these issues related to women's equality? I will discuss this issue by using a report from *China Daily* in 2000, a book called *Equality and Development* edited by Li Xiaojing 1997 (she is the chief editor of a series of books about gender issues), and a handbook from the conference *Expert Workshop On Fighting Domestic Violence Against Women: Social, Ethical, and Legal Issues,* Beijing 1997.

An August 4, 2000, report in *China Daily,* "Chinese Faithful to Fidelity Idea," exposes how the Chinese people pushed marital legislation to punish the increasing incidence of bigamy or *bao ernai* ("keeping a second wife" in Cantonese). According to this report, a survey conducted by the All China Women's

Federation (ACWF) in spring 2000 in several provinces such as Beijing, Hebei, Hubei, and Guangdong covered topics including marriage procedures, domestic violence, spouse rape, and divorce. Among these issues, the most controversial one is *bao ernai*. This practice has become more common in some prosperous regions in southern districts of Guangdong province. In the ACWF survey, 75 percent of the people said that the law should criminalize extramarital sex, which is not punishable by current legislation. It is interesting to note that the survey found that some 78 percent of women, 5 percentage points more than men, said extramarital sex should be a punishable offense. Why have women looked less tolerantly than men on this practice? Simply, women are the victims, and men are the beneficiaries. Regarding the idea of marital fidelity, women would be more supportive of this idea, since women depend upon it more than men, who have more choices in their control (e. g., being financially capable of supporting their mistresses).

In this report, Hu Kangsheng, the deputy director of the Legislative Affairs Commission under the National People's Congress, condemned *bao ernai* as "a social evil." According to him, it not only undermined social ethics, but also threatened social stability (family breakups, suicide, etc.). However, the law cannot eradicate this evil because some mistresses are kept under the pretense of being secretaries or maids, so that men can escape punishment for bigamy. In addition, 8 percent of the people believed extramarital love is only a kind of emotional connection and does not jeopardize family life and so is not a threat or evil to social stability.

Whether the practice of keeping mistresses is a social evil or not is not my present concern. What I am concerned with is the issue of who keeps whom. It is clearly shown that "overseas businessmen, corporate managers and some government officials have been found keeping mistresses."[9] These keepers happen to be men, powerful men to those mistresses or second wives. An obvious relationship between the dominated and the subordinated is the meaning of this practice. These second wives definitely cannot have a sense of equal respect, and no sense of their own dignity. In this social phenomenon of *bao ernai*, women retreat from the social ideal of gender equality and are looked down upon as means to satisfy men's sexual desires. The report also mentioned that 96 percent of the people in the survey thought the marriage law should outlaw domestic violence. I will move to this issue next.

I came to know domestic violence early in the 1970s when I settled down in Shanxi province during the Cultural Revolution. I realized that teenage children in the village were not allowed to choose partners but arranged to marry by parents according to how much bride money they could get for their son's bride. Some girls were lucky to be treated well when they got married. Some were treated as an object bought at an expensive price. Two decades later, domestic violence was openly discussed in women studies programs and conferences. I will comment on a survey conducted by Xu Anqi, who addresses this issue by blaming women.

Xu claims that her survey provides a different perspective from others that usually used accusers (almost all of them were women) as the objects of their survey. Xu chose ordinary couples as her research subjects, and her survey focused on 500 couples in the city of Shanghai in 1987, and 1670 couples in both the city and the suburbs of Shanghai in 1990. Through her survey, Xu found that one-third of couples committed violence during their arguments and it seemed mainly husbands beating wives, rather than the other way around, wives beating husbands. This is consistent with a global feminist observation that women are the victims of domestic violence. Nevertheless, Xu points out that it may not be true that the increasing rate of divorce is due to the husband's violence, even though many wives say so in order to win their suits. From this unusual perspective, Xu gives an analysis of cultural and psychological grounds for domestic violence.

Xu states that women's arrogance and self-will could cause and increase conflicts between couples, and even could lead to violence, although women were the victims. She gives several cultural and psychological reasons as follows. First, women in Shanghai were not following the role of virtuous wives and rejected their roles as feudalist ideas, often taking domineering attitudes toward their husbands and tempting their husbands to beat them. Second, women had double burdens and more responsibilities than men for the family, and hence, they felt unequal to men psychologically. These women liked to use offensive words to attack their husbands, and so husbands would be hurt and immediately use their cuff and kick. Third, some women were narrow-minded and garrulous. They were hypersensitive and had a good memory for details of minor things, which men could not match. These women's complaining would never end during family arguments. Their husbands' tolerance had limitations and they would lose patience with their wives' endless garrulity.[10]

These charges against women of not being virtuous and humble, but too arrogant and complaining too much, were used as justifications for men's violence against women. Such charges indicate Xu's position of supporting women's traditional roles and hence the male-dominated family. Obviously, her statement of women's arrogance as the cause of domestic conflicts can only count as a partial external cause of the violence. What is the internal cause of domestic violence? She does not explore this at all. Why could these men not control their tempers when their wives complained too much? Why did they choose violence rather than other options?

Xu's discussion of the origins of domestic violence (her charge that it stems in part from women's arrogance) implies her endorsement of the traditional norms of women's behavior such as humility, which is based on assumptions of sex difference. According to those assumptions, men are naturally aggressive and women are humble and tolerant. If women's position improved and they began to be more active and powerful than before, the relationship of husband and wife would be unbalanced and cause a husband's cuffs and kicks, as Xu states. This statement is absurd and invalid because it comes from the assumptions of sex difference and gender inequality in traditional stereotyped norms. Also, it is unjust to blame the victim of domestic violence.

As associate professor in women studies at Shanghai Academy of Social Sciences, Xu expressed some popular opinions about women's liberation. Her view that women are not the only victims of domestic violence is a good point, because it brings to light the fact that men could be victims too. The purpose of opposing domestic violence from the viewpoint of feminism is not just because it is a criminal offense, but also because it reflects a gender issue: why are females more likely to be victims than men, not the other way around? Xu simply did not explore this question.

A woman scholar, Jin Yihong, suggests that there is a need to change the existing social structure of power relationships in which male dominates female. Jin also criticizes that the charge that women are the cause of men's violence (because women are garrulous) is one kind of cultural worship of violence. This denunciation of the victims cannot help uncover the real cause of the violence but blurs the issue of sex discrimination and punishment of the weak. Domestic violence is not just an issue of criminal behavior, but also an issue of how people think of sex/gender relations. The violence has its root in discrimination against women: sexism caused violence (Jin 1997).

Such sexism and worship of power also appears in the issue of marital rape, which was brought up by some male feminist thinkers, Li Dun and Pan Suimin, in the expert workshop, Beijing, 1997. There are many case studies about family abuse of wives (Wang Xingjuan 1997), and most research suggests that educating men to treat women with respect and dignity would solve this problem. However, little research has addressed a question that is both legal and moral: whether a rape is committed or not if a husband forces his wife to have sex?

Under the state policy of protecting women, there were two movements, in the 1950s and 1980s, to punish husbands for the conviction of abusing women, but no mention of marital rape (Li Dun 1997b, 337). Rape could happen outside marriage, but it disappeared in marriage according to the explanation of criminal law experts. In Li's interpretation, the state law after 1997 changed the definition of rape from "an offense against decency" to "a violation against a person's right," but it does not explore the issue of rape within marriage, and it leaves such rape in an ambiguous status (330-31). According to the mainstream legal view, rape exists only outside marital relationships because Chinese culture adopts "the principle of collective interests" (338) which is beyond any regulation of formal laws. This principle requires individual obligations rather than rights. Most Chinese women would be wives, and wives should respond to their husbands' desires for sex because of women's obligations, hence, women's rights to say no disappear in such cultural endorsement.

Li Dun notes that people's attitudes toward the issue of marital rape are changing, since the emergence of feminist critical challenges to cultural institutions against women. He also asks a question: "Have men gotten individual rights similar to what women should seek?" (1997b, 341). Li realizes that Chinese law does not give a clear explanation of what is a person's right in his (her) sexuality, and how the law should intervene when one's rights and obligations conflict with each other. The law got left behind in the fast-changing Chinese society in the period of economic transformation. Li does not suggest how it should be changed to deal with marital rape. However, he certainly argues that marital rape exists and that the law should intervene in this offense. The other scholar, Pan (1997), further discusses this issue.

Pan emphasizes that both women and men should have equal sexual rights, but he asks a question to remind us of how far we should go to defend those rights: can we be tolerant and accept freedom of sex without marriage, homosexual behavior, and uncoerced prostitutes? Pan has drawn a new perspective from which to see the issue: sexual rights only matter for the protection of the weak, and women would be likely to depend upon and be sympathetic toward those rights of protection. Men would not be worried about sexual rights, since their dominance in every aspect of social life enables their enjoyment of rights (1997, 85-86). From Pan's view, we can draw a point that boys also should be protected from sexual abuse and also men from sexual assault. Men and women should have equal rights in sex practice.

All the above discussions of sexuality and domestic violence are related to a fundamental question of sex difference and similarity, and why inequality between men and women has persisted so long and been so stubbornly clung to by Chinese society.

Comments on Equal Opportunity

Women's subordinated situations in the post-Mao era have brought into question the traditional view of women's virtues and different sex roles. On the other hand, the sex/gender sameness of Mao's time is out of date and never really worked. Encountering the rapid changes in women's situations and the decline in women's status, Chinese feminists have been puzzled about how to pursue the social ideal of women's equality. Chinese feminists realize that the idea of equal opportunity does not help women promote their status if it only means equal competition in the rapid economic development without taking into account real inequalities in opportunity for different groups of Chinese women. The revival of the Confucian view of women's proper roles and new opportunities for women's development put double-role expectations on women and increased their double burdens. The Confucian view of women emphasizes the innate difference of sexes, and so legitimates sex roles, which have never been seriously examined during the revolutionary movements. I will discuss Western feminist insights on the issue of sex roles and sex difference in order to clarify what kind of equality Chinese women need. I will argue that the current version of equal opportunity is only "formal" equality of opportunity, but Chinese women need a more substantive equality of opportunity. I will argue that Chinese women still need the state policy of protecting women by a contrast with affirmative action in the United States.

Why have people persisted in believing that there are inherent natural roles for men and women even if they know that sex roles are the product of socialization rather than naturalization? Ferguson gives a convincing answer to this question: "Sex-role ideologies mystify the existing power relations between men and women and economic classes. This mystification justifies the social and economic roles of two dominant groups: men as a caste, on the one hand, and the dominant economic class on the other" (1991, 198).

Thus, some feminists advocate the idea of androgyny rather than sex difference. The discussion of androgyny can be summarized as follows: we need a new model of human development; what a good person is like rather than what a woman is like or what a man is like. A good society should present a variety of opportunities for a person's free choice, and sexual equality is the necessary condition for implementing this new model and a neutral standard for a good person and a good society. The first step for androgyny supporters is to criticize the sex stereotypes by exposing their invalid arguments.

Joyce Trebilcot has shown three major ways in which the claims have been made that natural differences between the sexes underlie sex roles, that sex roles are inevitable, and that sex roles are efficient. None of them are valid, according to her arguments.

The advocates of inevitable sex roles hold that if there are innate psychological differences between females and males, sex roles are inevitable. But, as Trebilcot states, even if we accept the premises that the natural behavioral differences are inevitable, does it follow that there must be sex roles, that is, the social institutions must enforce correlations between roles and sex? Surely not! Why bother to direct women into some roles and men into others if the pattern occurs regardless of the nature of society (Trebilcot 1982, 44). John Stuart Mill makes this point very elegantly in *The Subjection of Women,* as Trebilcot describes: "The anxiety of mankind to interfere in behalf of nature, for fear lest nature should not succeed in effecting its purpose, is an altogether unnecessary solicitude" (44).

The second argument for sex roles claims that, because of natural psychological differences between the sexes, the members of each sex are happier in certain roles than in others, and roles that tend to promote happiness are different for each sex. In addition, if all roles are equally available to everyone, it is possible for some individuals to choose against their own well-being, hence, for the sake of maximizing well-being, there should be sex roles: the society should encourage individuals to make "correct" role choices. Trebilcot points out, that the conclusion of this argument needs to add another assumption, that is, the loss of the potential well-being resulting from socially-engineered adoption of unsuitable roles by some individuals is less than the loss that would result from "mistaken" free choices if there were no sex roles. But how do we know which system is better than the other? Surely, "we are not now in a position to compare the two systems with respect to the number of mismatches produced" (1982, 46). Hence, the conclusion that overall well-being is greater with sex roles than without them is entirely unsustainable.

The third argument is concerned with efficiency: in order to save time and effort for proficiency training, we do better to select the more talented than the less talented. If there are natural differences between the sexes in their capacity to perform socially valuable tasks, then efficiency is served if these tasks are assigned to the sex with the greatest innate ability for them. This conclusion, too, is weak when compared with the arguments against sex roles, according to Trebilcot, because in order to determine whether there should be sex roles, one would have to weigh efficiency, together with other reasons for such roles, against reasons for holding that there should not be sex roles, yet these reasons "are very coached in terms of individual rights—in terms of liberty, justice, equality of opportunity." Therefore, "Efficiency by itself does not outweigh these moral values" (1982, 47).

All these arguments in support of the view that there should be sex roles are based on a presupposition of natural psychological differences between men and women. This is a presumption made by all male-centered cultures, but it is unjustified because we are not in the position to know whether these sex differences are natural or not.

In her book *Making All the Difference* (1990), Martha Minow explores "The Dilemma of Difference." She uses examples to explain this term: In bilingual and special education programs, schools struggle to deal with students defined as "different" without stigmatizing them. In both contexts, it is a difficult task to remedy inequality. If schools treat people differently by emphasizing differences, this different treatment would stigmatize or hinder these people on that basis. On the other hand, treating people the same would be insensitive to their differences and likely to stigmatize or hinder them on that basis. This dilemma applies to many situations beyond school. For example, women have special needs such as maternity leave in the workplace. Are women merely helped or hurt? Are their biological differences from men accommodated in this fulfillment of the vision of equality? Or are negative stereotypes reinforced in violation of commitments to equality? Minow suggests that the dilemma of difference is not just an accidental problem in society. It grows from the ways in which society assigns people to categories: the assigned categories based on age, race, gender, and so on, have been used to determine who gets included and who does not (1990, 20-21). Minow analyzes critically several unstated assumptions behind the dilemma of difference: difference is intrinsic, not a comparison; norms need not be stated; the observer can see without a perspective; and other perspectives are irrelevant. All these unstated entities make the dilemma of difference seem intractable. However, if they were exposed and debated, it would open room for new solutions. The new approaches should reconsider the relationships and patterns of power that influence the negative consequences of difference and explore new possibilities for change. According to Minow, attention to relationships between groups and the power constructed through those relationships leads us to see the importance of the context in which a particular trait of difference comes to matter. The social-relations approach is interested in context and stresses actual social experiences and their meanings to the people involved rather than abstract or formal principles (1990, 117).

Minow also argues that feminist challenges to the ethics of care will go further to query differences in power instead of just deepening an interest in "care" or "responsibility." According to her, only through relational themes can feminist methodologies frame the issues in ways that avoid those constraining assumptions behind the dilemma of difference. Hence, feminists urge the recasting of issues of differences as problems of dominance or subordination. They urge that we locate differences within relationships of differential power and disclose the social relationship or power within the way difference is named and enforced. The analysis of how difference is named and assigned in relationships or power further questions implicit norms; norms based on the male experience become a subject for contest. Rather than assuming that women must adjust to a workplace designed for men, we can advocate a desirable workplace designed for both men and women (1990, 218). Through all the above analyses, the idea of an unsituated perspective on issues of difference fails to address the influence of the observer on the observed. Only the relational approach can do the job of disclosing differences and raise the hope of getting out of the dilemma of difference.

Minow's and other feminist insights are very helpful for Chinese women trying to recognize their roles and development. The model of equal opportunity does not help women if society encourages double expectations and different gender roles for women but a single expectation and role for men. It seems that the idea of women's equality became unpopular because of the fact of women's double burdens, conflicting heavily loaded lives, and the continuing inequality of social arrangements between genders. Without a thorough understanding of these power inequalities, as exposed in Minow's work, Chinese women can hardly challenge the revival of the Confucian view of sex roles and difference.

The impediment to increased equality falsely led people, especially women, to turn back to the traditional views of women, rather than to a modern view of themselves as self-governing people. This backwardness in women's status, in my view, does not prove the wrongness of the social ideal of equality, but the complication, dilemma, difficulty, and toughness involved in seeking this ideal.

I suggest that the state should protect women by a policy similar to affirmative action (AA) in the United States and continue its promise for women's equality. AA has always been controversial in the United States. It is historically associated with Title VII of the Civil Rights Act of 1964. The Civil Rights Act prohibits discrimination on the basis of race, sex, and so on, by private as well as public employers. "Title VII of the Act and its associated strategy of affirmative action are today the United States' most powerful legal instruments for countering employment discrimination on the basis of sex" (Jaggar 1995a, 73). Here, I will skip all charges of AA resulting in reverse discrimination and focus on feminist challenges to AA.

Catharine MacKinnon criticizes that AA fails to offer a fundamental challenge to the existing male norms and standards of merit, and even reinforces the male-biased institutions. She writes:

> Virtually every quality that distinguishes men from women is already affirmatively compensated in this society. Men's physiology defines most sports, their needs define auto and health insurance coverage, their socially designed biographies define workplace expectations and successful career patterns, their perspectives and concerns define quality in scholarship, their experiences and obsessions define merit . . . For each of their differences from women, what amounts to an affirmative action plan is in effect, otherwise known as the structures and values of American society. (MacKinnon 1987, 36)

These statements sharply point out that AA programs fundamentally are grounded in traditional conceptualizations of achievements and social organizations. However, as Jaggar responds, MacKinnon's argument to the conservative consequences of AA is "overly pessimistic." Despite the fundamental limitation of AA, "The inclusion of more women—like MacKinnon herself—in professions such as law, medicine, psychotherapy, and academia in fact has encouraged increasing challenges to definitions of reality that favor men" (Jaggar 1995, 97). This thought is supported by Laura Purdy, who is questioning definitions that are male-biased and need to be rethought (Purdy 1994).

Through these comments on the social consequences of AA, we see the contradictory aspects of AA programs: "it simultaneously undermines as well as reinforces the male-defined *status quo*" (Jaggar 1995a, 98).

Jaggar further advances a question of AA and sex equality. According to her observation, after thirty years of AA, it seems that young middle-class women in the United States are closer to equality in employment than were their mothers, but the situation of many working-class women (most of them women of color) has deteriorated. If this is the case, who is going to take care of the interests of working-class women?

Although full equality of employment opportunity for women requires a wide range of measures, as suggested by Jaggar (1995a, 100-102), AA can play a part in the transition toward equality of opportunity, despite problems in practice in its programs. I will move to contrast AA with the state policy to help women in the post-Mao period. Have Chinese women still the need for the state policy of antidiscrimination of women in employment? Considering all the inequalities between men and women exposed in previous sections and the failure of equal opportunity to promote women's equality, and the rehabilitation of Confucianism, I would say Chinese women still need state protection, but what does the state need to do to improve women's equality in a new period of economic transformation? I will discuss that in the next chapter.

I also see great hope coming from discussions of the current situation of Chinese women's inequality: the more perplexed women feel about their lives, the more conscious thinking about their subordination will emerge. The feminist perspective will help Chinese women examine the traditional view of women and challenge all theories that rationalize women's inequalities and subordinations. The examination should go beyond merely economic aspects and add a critical analysis of the sex/gender system, which is crucial to clarifying the issue of women's oppression. Although I doubt that a one-dominant-party ruling state like China would allow women and feminists to make any fundamental challenges to the dominant male-centered ideology—which is supported by the existing social structure of sexism—I desire an open-door policy to developing democracy and helping women make progress toward full equality. In the next chapter, I will develop my view of women's equality in the twenty-first century, which must be women-centered and prioritize empowerment.

Notes

1. Wang Qi, "State-Society Relations and Women's Political Participation," in *Women of China: Economic and Social Transformation*, ed. Jackie West (New York: St. Martin's Press, 1999), 19-44.

2. Cadres are officials working for the government. They never have to worry about unemployment, although their salaries are moderate compared with those of business managers in companies.

3. Zhang Heather Xiaoquan, "Understanding Changes in Women's Status in the Context of the Recent Rural Reform," in *Women of China: Economic and Social Transformation*, ed. Jackie West (New York: St. Martin's Press, 1999), 45-66.

4. Huang Xiyi, "Divided Gender, Divided Women: State Policy and the Labor Market," in *Women of China: Economic and Social Transformation*, ed. Jackie West (New York: St. Martin's Press, 1999), 90.

5. Song Lina, "The Role of Women in Labor Migration: A Case Study in Northern China," in *Women of China: Economic and Social Transformation*, ed. Jackie West (New York: St. Martin's Press, 1999), 74.

6. Family breaks include legal divorce or permanent separation, e.g. the wife remains in a village while her husband has a second wife in his working place.

7. Wang Xingjuan, the head of the first women's hotline in China, supported by the Ford Foundation since 1992.

8. *Xiangtu Zhongguo* (*From the Soil: The Foundations of Chinese Society*, 1992) is one of the most influential works of contemporary social studies in China. The author, Fei Xiaotong (President of the Society of Sociology of China), was awarded the 1980 B. Malinowski Honorary Prize by the International Applied Anthropology Association, won the Huxley Memorial Medal given by the Royal Anthropological Institute of Great Britain and Ireland, and received other honors. See Wolfgang Bartke, *Who's Who in the People's Republic of China* (1991), 120-21.

9. "Chinese Faithful to Fidelity Idea," *China Daily*, August 4, 2000.

10. Xu Anqi, "The Origins of Domestic Violence in Cities," in Li Xiaojiang, *Equality and Development: Studies of Gender and China*, vol. 2 (Beijing: Sanlian Bookstore, 1997), 266-67.

Chapter Five

A Democratic Conception of Women's Equality

My examination of several twentieth-century views of the ideal relations between men and women in China reveals that all can be used to rationalize the subordination of women. The Confucian view of women fails to help women promote their status as equal with men; and three models of equality—formal, substantive, and equal opportunity—although necessary, are still insufficient for achieving full equality.

In this chapter I will sketch a new model of sex equality, which is distinguished by being nonessentialist and inclusive of women's different voices. This model can utilize the Western feminist vision of critical care, but it will also draw on valuable resources in the Chinese tradition: the Confucian idea of the relational self and the Maoist state policy of giving women special protections. This sounds like a dilemma since a top-down state policy may control and prevent a self-motivated pursuit of equality, and therefore might damage a democratic model for seeking equality. I will argue that Chinese feminists cannot copy the Western model of democracy completely because of the characteristics of Chinese culture, history, and tradition, and the ways in which these currently influence every aspect of Chinese women's lives. I propose a gradual progress toward a democratic model of full equality—a transformation from semi-democracy to complete democracy and equality for women. In order to understand this democratic concept, we must retain a critical view of the Chinese tradition, a vision of this democratic model, and a vision of how this model can promote women's power in political, economic, and all social opportunities through their different voices.

In order to decide which parts of Confucianism and Maoism are valuable for people to claim, and which parts are harmful to the social ideals of democracy and equality, I will discuss the following themes. First, I argue that the core of a democratic conception of sexual equality should be women who are self-directed rather than state-directed. Women must be conscious subjects rather than passive objects in seeking the ideal of equality. Second, I will emphasize that the self-directed model needs to highlight women's consciousness about their oppression as females. This is particularly important in the current stage of economic development in China—what matters in seeking sexual equality is not just material or economic conditions but the recognition of gender-consciousness as Ferguson advocates. Third, I will examine the question, raised by Hall and Ames, of whether Confucianism can be taken as a democratic vision and adapted into a democratic model of women's equality through the ideal of reciprocity, a golden rule in Confucianism. I argue that this rule is not equally effective in women's experiences because of the notion of women's special virtues prescribed by Confucianism. Fourth, I will continue to argue for the state policy of supporting women's participation in economic development by helping women's autonomy and raising their gender consciousness. The state's special help for women should not be the dominant mode of representing all women but should help women voice their own needs. This is crucial in developing my democratic model through the discussion of various nongovernmental organizations (NGOs) in China during the Fourth World Conference on Women in 1995 and their cooperation with a government that commits to gender equality on the surface of their official words. The last theme in my reconception of equality for women will focus on how to empower women by including their different voices. I will compare the idea of parity of effective voice from Jaggar with Chinese women's situations and offer concrete suggestions for ways to include women's voices through programs promoting gender-consciousness. I begin by explaining the need for this democratic conception, then discuss the above themes, and finally focus on women's empowerment.

The Need for a Democratic Model of Women's Equality

What is the common problem in the various Chinese feminist pursuits of women's equality in the last century? In chapter 1, I argued that the Confucian view of women rationalized women's inequality because the idea of *ren*, as a supreme virtue, is thought attainable by women only in a distinctively feminine form—by obedience and subordination. During the May Fourth Movement, the Western model of formal equality emerged along with other social thoughts in China, and the rebellious spirit against Confucianism joined the fight with the nationalist, communist, and feminist struggles against women's oppression. However, the feminist idea of liberal formal equality is not sufficient to confront the vital issues of national survival and Chinese people's livelihood. The turbulent wartime situation obstructed the development of women's equality, and feminists were suppressed by the autocratic government. In Mao's time, the ideal of substantive equality became the official state approach to promoting women's positions in production and other areas of society. However, Mao's substantive equality as a state control and dominant voice, together with his political centralization, prevented women from exploring such issues as double burdens, personal happiness, and sexuality. Mao's model of equality is insufficient for women to attain their own goals in seeking equality. In the post-Mao era, because of the rapid development of a market economy and the state's complete retreat from policies favoring women, an extremely harsh backlash against women's equality is occurring. The market itself does not promote sex equality—it strengthens sex inequality by fostering an illusion of equal economic opportunity regardless of sex. In addition, a revival of the traditional view of women advocates that women's proper role is to assist men, family, and society. The double expectation on women but not on men increases women's burdens and causes women to be less competitive than men in terms of equal opportunity. Because women have special needs and interests, any models of equality ignoring these needs fail to address the issue of equality for women. Thus, formal economic opportunity cannot help women achieve true equality.

All four models of the relationship between women and men used at various times in China have a common feature in different forms—a lack of democracy for women. The undeveloped ideal of formal equality for women was suppressed by reactionary authority. The substantive equality of production improved women's status by the top-down policy while this top-down policy kept women in silence and muted their own interests. The idea of equal economic opportunity is also a top-down policy in the rapid economic transition period, and it lacks a thorough exploration of what would make women's opportunities truly equal. Without an enhanced democratic discussion of the prerequisite material for realizing sex equality, the model of equal opportunity did not help women but resulted in the feminization of agriculture and feminization of poverty.

All these conceptions of women's equality tried to either protect or instruct women through top-down policies or ideologies that were supposed to take care of women's needs and desires. In fact, they continued women's subordination and oppression, because they could not represent what women actually needed. Women's equality should not be imposed on women by any external authority, but should be sought by women themselves. Without independent thinking by women concerning their own status and without fundamentally challenging institutionalized male domination, women never can attain equality in systematically sexist societies.

Chinese women need a new model, a democratic model of how to seek their equality and emancipation in the new era of globalization. What should a democratic conception of women's equality be and how is it distinctively different from past models? I would like to use a comment from Sue Mansfield's introduction to *The Subjection of Women* as a ground for this model:

> Again and again [Mill] makes the point that until women themselves are involved in the investigation and until more attention is paid to the problem of the influence of society upon individual development, then anything which is said about women remains simply a matter of opinion and prejudice. (Mill 1980, xxiii)

Democracy and Sex Equality

In this section, I will argue that a democratic model of sex equality should be motivated by two principal aspects: one is gender awareness or consciousness; the other is opposing top-down ideologies. I will discuss two issues related to these aspects—first the intrinsic value of democracy as a key to raise Chinese women's gender-consciousness, and second, the Confucian notion of reciprocity as not accountable for women's equality but as a rationale for their subordination.

A new model of a democratic conception of women's equality must pay great attention to what women's real needs and interests are, and be aware that women's special needs and interests are not all the same. This model should be distinctive in its democratic approach that is based on including the voices of differently situated women. In order to reach this goal, the democratic model must emphasize the intrinsic value of self-government.

A democratic model of equality must commit to the value of democracy— regard democracy as an "end in itself," an intrinsic value as opposed to just an "instrumental" value (Cunningham 2002, 149). The classic view of democracy involves self-government. Classic liberalism considers that all people have the ability to use reason to make their own decisions and that their self-determination for personal development should be the ultimate value. From this view it follows that women should have the same natural right to make choices and develop themselves (Ferguson 1991, 165). Hence, democracy and women's equality require each other. Since self-determination requires one's comprehensive knowledge and ability to make independent decisions, "democracy" seems to be a luxury condition unavailable to vulnerable people. When democracy is applied to Chinese women (more than half of whom cannot read and write), it is much more difficult to follow its theoretical notions. Nevertheless, undemocratic approaches to sex equality like Mao's top-down policy did not really work to achieve women's equality. Chinese women should begin with a self-motivated seeking of equality and all women workers, scholars, and policy makers should help women with the idea of promoting women's self-government and self-determining pursuit of equality.

In her book *Sexual Democracy* (1991), Ferguson also regarded China as a failed experiment in sexual equality during the socialist transformation because of its underdeveloped, peasant society. She chose Eastern European industrial societies, such as East Germany, and argued that because of certain socialist programs, women there were comparatively better off than women in the United States. In this analysis, Ferguson points out that an undeveloped country like China has two problems in providing gender equality programs: its peasant culture is more patriarchal and has seriously limited resources available for socializing domestic work, and it lacks the material resources to free women from the male-controlled economy (Ferguson 1991, 162).

Ferguson makes a great point: sexual equality and women's liberation require multidimensional struggles of the political, economic, and cultural, rather than one single struggle. Women must have the material resources to free themselves from domestic burdens and also the political resources to eliminate male domination and power in the state and family. But improving women's material base itself is not just an economic issue. In the model of democratic equality, feminists should pay great attention to the inseparable connections between different modes of women's oppression because they are situated differently from men.

The two problems in China, as Ferguson states—the strong patriarchy and weak material resources—make it quite difficult to provide sexual equality programs. However, this does not mean that a single strategy, rebelling either against the patriarchy or against rapid economic change, could easily increase sexual equality. The view that "the economy will not permit [sex equality]" also harms sexual equality programs.[1] Women should not wait for their economic level to advance to gain equal opportunities. Women's equality can only be attained by women's own actions through step-by-step progress. Women should strive to be involved in economic development, and feminists cannot expect that economic perks for women will be handed out through top-down policies but should fight for women's participation in the market and share in the outcome of economic changes. The democratic model of sexual equality encourages feminists to simultaneously pursue political, cultural, and economic equality; it encourages women to act immediately to alter their inequality through their own involvement.

The second issue for gender-consciousness-raising in the model of democratic equality is the epistemic one. The long history of Chinese peasant culture has nurtured the strongest patriarchal authority in the state and family. The Confucian idea of *ren* (benevolence or supreme humanity) became common sense rather than a mere academic value, and most Chinese deal with each other through the Confucian principle of reciprocity. Should the model of democratic sexual equality use this traditional ethical maxim to promote women's status? In order to clarify this issue, gender-consciousness analysis should be inculcated into that ethical golden rule.[2]

In *The Democracy of the Dead* (1999), Hall and Ames defend Confucius's view as a democratic theory because they think it is compatible with American Deweyan[3] pragmatism. They find common features between Confucianism and pragmatism. Hall and Ames write, "Equality, construed in individualistic terms, is a quantitative notion." According to them, because "the definition of persons as autonomous individuals militates against the notion of goods held in common," such a notion does a poor job of maintaining order. In terms of the relational self, the Confucian community likes an extended family with resolutely hierarchical relations, but these roles and relations are reciprocal: "The roles of communal benefactor and beneficiary alternate over time. Hierarchy need not be as rigid and inflexible as it is often thought to be" (160). They even go further to suggest that the resources within Confucian classics could be used to promote equality for women and minorities, even for overcoming gender inequality!

Here, the issue is whether hierarchy can be coexistent with democracy, especially in women's situations. The defenders of Confucian hierarchy use the notion of reciprocity to justify unequal roles. In practice, reciprocal relationships do not occur between ruler and subjects, or husband and wife, where the hierarchy is rigid and inflexible. Nevertheless, Hall and Ames insist: "Confucianism offers important, largely unused, resources for overcoming gender inequities" (1999, 161). They give evidence for this claim from two sides. One is the lesson of liberal rights-based democracy. The Western means of becoming truly human perpetuates the old male prerogatives. As they say, "To be fully human you must be (largely) male." The other is the merit of Confucian and pragmatist equality, a qualitative notion, which refers to one's self-cultivation. A self-realized person can be defined in terms of a dynamic balance of yin and yang characteristics (201).

What does Hall and Ames's qualitative notion of equality mean for women? It is hard to find an explicit analysis. According to them, the Confucian conception of the individual is dynamic, entailing that one is identified by a complex of social roles. "It is the quality of these roles that focuses one's identity, which is constitutive of one's self." They go on to claim that such a conception of a person as a specific matrix of roles "will not tolerate any assertion of natural equality" and that in it a "person [is] understood in irrevocably hierarchical relationships that reflect fundamental differences among them" (1999, 198).

With a strong sense of fundamental differences and hierarchy in mind, how could the qualitative notion of equality work toward a sense of equality at a high level? Hall and Ames explain: First, the dynamic nature of roles means that privileges and duties within one's community tend to last for a lifetime, rather than a short time; second, one's duties and privileges can be balanced through changing one's roles, e.g., a son's duties will be balanced by his privileges as a parent; similarly one's role as benefactor during middle years will be paid back when one grows old. Therefore, they conclude, "A dynamic field of relationships over time produces a degree of parity in what is perceived as the most vital source of humanity—one's human relations" (1999, 198).

According to the above argument for qualitative equality between people, all that matters is the reciprocity of dynamic relationships and nothing beyond that. However, first, in the notion of reciprocity, one's roles tend to last for a lifetime, which does not sound very dynamic. Second, in the relationship of supreme ruler and the inferior ruled, it is supposed that the ruled must always play loyal roles to the ruler in order to be protected. This hierarchy is rigid and inflexible enough to oppress the powerless ruled. By no means could the ruled resist an abusive authority. There is no reciprocity in these relationships since the hierarchy does not tolerate any equality between the two. The powerful superior class benefits from this relationship.

Similar situations occurred between wives and husbands: the rigid sex roles and the division of labor regulated each sex playing their roles appropriately. Most women played their roles best during the so-called "golden age." But that did not mean that they would be protected when they grew old, as we see from women's situations exposed by He in chapter 4. There was no reciprocal relationship: The qualitative service of young wives as benefactor did not guarantee that qualitative service was paid back when they got old. Why is a woman most likely the benefactor rather than a beneficiary? No satisfactory explanation can be found in Hall and Ames's argument about how to achieve real equality of the sexes in women's relevant situations, as they only describe the "fundamental differences among them."

The other response to the reciprocity theory could be worse: it seems that the ruler and the ruled might take turns in oppressing and being oppressed. If we look at the history of Chinese peasant uprisings against despotic rulers, if the peasants won, the new ruler continued to oppress the ruled. These features of oppression and inequality remained in so-called reciprocity relationships, which are far removed from modern ideas of equality and democracy.[4]

In the above examination of the application of reciprocity in women's experiences as wife and mother, it is obvious that there is a power imbalance between men and women, which is justified by the Confucian cosmology of yin-yang theory (see Dong Zhongshu in chapter 1), and compatible with the Confucian view of women's three-fold obedience. Noting this power inequality in applying the rule of reciprocity to women, feminists should first of all delete the stereotyped beliefs of valuing females differently from males. If both genders are equally concerned and respected, the reciprocity rule will work in a flexible way—women and men can choose different social roles freely according to their own determination. No top-down ideology should prescribe fixed roles for one sex rather than the other. Hence, both men and women can be benefactors and beneficiaries in accordance with their free choices.

When women understand the way in which power inequality between the sexes occurred in the past and was supported by stereotyped views of sex roles, this new reciprocity without sex discrimination can become reality. Gender-consciousness is crucial to analyzing the roots of women's oppression as members of the female sex, and enhancing sex analysis of the issue of reciprocity will help women critically accept the traditional golden rule but reject its feature of sex discrimination.

What Counts as a Democratic Model of Sex Equality?

In the previous two sections I discussed two features of a new conception of sexual equality—its democratic emphasis on women's self-determination, and its gender-consciousness. In this section, I will discuss its openness and evolving nature. I adopt a view of "Democracy is a matter of degree" drawn from Dewey's approach (Cunningham 2002, 144). Since democracy and equality require each other, and both of them demand continuing progress toward their full realization, I emphasize openness in each pursuit. This openness guarantees women will find their voices and enhances a democratic search for women's equality. This openness should exist in the following three aspects—NGO discourses, the cooperation of different NGOs, and exchange activities between the domestic and the international.[5] I will use Wesoky's investigation of the above three aspects and draw a slightly different conclusion from hers.

Here I need to clarify the difference between what I mean by openness in the democratic model of equality and the open-door policy of the Communist Party. The openness in my model is a kind of unlimited inclusion of different voices concerning women's issues, and it should give equal concern and respect to all different opinions as long as they express women's special needs and interests. Because of its attention to the voices of women at the bottom, it differs from the top-down policy, which is limited to the party's dominant voice. The open-door policy can benefit women; however, they should be vigilant about the ideology's impact, because there is no reason to trust the ruling party to guard women's special needs, especially immigrant women's needs for jobs in big cities. On the other hand, the open-door policy is definitely necessary to achieve the above three aspects, various NGO organizations, and open discussions on women's issues.

Various NGOs and Their Cooperation

I would like to begin by answering the question, what does an NGO mean to Chinese women? Then I will discuss the cooperative relationship between Fulian (the All China Women's Federation), nongovernmental organizations (NGOs), other grass roots organizations, and their relations to the party-state. How to maintain cooperation is a new theme in the democratic conception of sex equality.

Chinese people did not know about NGOs until China started its preparatory process for the Fourth World Conference on Women (FWCW) after 1992. China was ranked 132nd in a world survey ranking women's status in various countries at a September 1988 international conference in Montreal (Wesoky 2002, 129). The Chinese government disagreed with this ranking and tried to change its world image by hosting the FWCW. As China prepared for the conference, the leaders emphasized its importance for China's place in the world. Chen Muhua, chairperson of the All China Women's Federation (ACWF), noted this, and she stated:

> We should promote our country's overall women's participation in development, in the process of realizing their own rights and interests. This conference also will be a great advancement for our country's friendly cooperation and exchanges with all countries of the world. (Chen Muhua 1994, 17)

The FWCW forced the Chinese government to confront the existence of NGOs during the one-year process of preparing for the conference, but the process also led to an important shift in Chinese thinking on NGOs. The state attempted to exert its control over the preparatory process, while Fulian was entrusted with much of the work. The state stressed that Fulian was to follow the leadership of the party and government. However, the process of organizing the event forced Fulian to make its own identity shift, leading it to calling itself an NGO (Wesoky 2002, 173).

Why did Fulian want to become an NGO? First, Fulian leadership became aware that NGOs are not illegal (they are not willing to oppose the government) and can maintain harmony with the government. Second, and most important, Fulian leadership realized that an NGO can represent women's interests and that serving those interests does not conflict with the state commitment to gender equality. Moreover, Fulian also saw that without NGO status, it could not attend the NGO forum, and NGOs are a direct force that international society should not be without. Thus, Fulian started to call itself an NGO. Although some people objected to an NGO representing the "official" viewpoint, Fulian is gradually entering an NGO role (Wesoky 2002, 173-74).

Wesoky enumerates eight characteristics that have commonly been regarded as important conditions for genuine NGO status in the Chinese women's movement: "financial independence, voluntarism, independence and freedom, 'looseness,' internal democracy, legality, diversity, and 'purity'" (2002, 177).

According to Wesoky's definition, Fulian barely meets these criteria. For instance, while NGOs have to struggle for funds, Fulian is supported by the government. However, in the "legality" category, other NGOs have support from some government units. To be a legal NGO in China, a group must both have a supervisory work unit and be registered with the relevant department of civil affairs. Therefore, NGOs are not necessarily AGOs (2002, 182) [AGO means "against government organization"]. Diversity in Chinese NGOs derives from three types of NGOs: There are the "traditional, half NGOs" such as Fulian because of its political color; the "academic" NGOs—university women studies centers; and "real, pure" new NGOs. However, "pure" NGOs are "very few in

China" and this type of NGO might succeed in establishing significant independence, yet remain within legal bounds (182).

In Wesoky's discussion, it seems that NGOs have varying degrees of social autonomy in China, and some groups claiming to be NGOs are really more "nongovernmental" than others. Some activists regard NGOs receiving foreign funding as a key factor in their increasing independence. "Pure" NGOs tend to be more interested in foreign ties than those under Fulian, and they more actively pursue international exchanges.

Here, I see a Western style of thinking about "independence" in the women's movement: the more ties with foreign resources and funds, the more independent from the Chinese government. Nonetheless, we have not investigated whether those international NGOs are "purely independent" or not. I have reservations about the view that "pure" NGOs are those which tend to be more interested in foreign ties than those under Fulian (Wesoky 2002, 183).

In Wesoky's conclusion, a worry about the absolute authority of the state is clearly shown: All Chinese NGOs have supervisory work units within the government apparatus, and they have to adopt a view of "nongovernmental organization" that stresses engaging in cooperation, rather than conflict (2002, 183). Thus, Wesoky argues that these NGOs could hardly fundamentally challenge the conceptual scheme of the state control ideology, because they are committed to cooperating with the state.

Wesoky is right to point out the state control that lies underneath the appearance of increasing organizational autonomy in Chinese NGO activities. I agree that NGO cooperation with the state prevents them from a deep pursuit of democracy—bottom-up self-determination rather than state top-down control. Nevertheless, the emergence of Chinese NGOs is the best chance of opening the Chinese women's movement to the global civil society, and the beginning of seeking a democratic conception of women's equality. Chinese feminists cannot expect full democracy as the starting point of democratic progress in the women's movement. Women engaged in NGOs must be able to establish a "legal" condition before they can start programs to help women, and they must have ties with the original work unit to get living necessities (usually housing and basic salaries). Once they lose ties with the work unit, these women scholars or activists would have no material base to continue their programs.

One may ask why these women did not fight in the first place against the government's regulation of NGOs. My answer is that women who accepted the party's policy of gender equality for four decades since the 1950s and feel confused about their status under the current economic changes may not be ready for radical action against a state that promises a policy of open doors and facing the world. Cooperating is better in China, for now, to keep a material base for women's causes.

Deepening Discussions by "Depoliticization"

As Wesoky described, in the process of preparing for the FWCW, Chinese women's movement activists learned a great deal about wider issues originating outside China, gained an increased sense of "the collective identity" of women, and gained in particular a great sense of their own agency. They realized commonalities with the international feminist movement and introduced new issues from abroad to a wider Chinese audience. Chinese feminist activists have taken advantage of the existing state commitment to gender equality to frame new issue agendas for gender-consciousness raising (Wesoky 2002, 185). The strategy of Chinese feminism used in cooperation with the state is "de-politicized" (193), rather than following the Western feminist strategy of "the personal is political."

Why do Chinese feminist scholars and activists choose a depoliticized attitude to frame new women's issues in the current economic changes? A women's studies scholar noted that:

> Before the conference the government had some fears. There was criticism from the West of governmental policies on women. Then after the conference the government saw that the criticism was of a social problem, not a governmental problem. So the government said you could discuss these things. (Wesoky 2002, 194)

The government believed that this political change in the status of women's issues would not hurt the government's image in regards to women's status. Thus the state adopted a more tolerant position regarding the discussion of women's issues. This also shows the state policy of increasing openness.

The list of issues that can now be discussed includes many sensitive topics. For example, prostitution was, in the past, a relatively closed topic; now prostitution and visiting prostitutes are openly reported. Other issues are the abduction and selling of women, domestic violence, women's reproductive health, marital rape, sexual harassment, etc. All these issues have been brought out through the cosponsored conferences or co-investigations of Fulian, NGOs, and grass roots activities. Fulian and NGO groups also run various training programs focused on counseling women in need (Wesoky 2002, 197).

The best example of the cooperation between various groups is the Ford-sponsored program in Reproductive Health and Ethics. This program lasted from 1993 to 1995, and was enhanced by including interdisciplinary decision-makers from the State Family Planning Commission and the Women's Federation, as well as journalists and researchers from academies of social science, universities, and NGOs. Not only did the program feature the creation of various "ethical principles" to guide policy making, but also included "action recommendation" in an effort to influence state policy and practice. Such a program relies on enthusiastic cooperation between various groups and experts, and its goal includes "making the formulation of reproductive health policies able to fully express women's opinions and voices" (Wesoky 2002, 210).

Wesoky raises an interesting question about the Reproductive Health Program: Why would the Chinese state allow such a program, with its seeming challenges to state authority, to be instituted in the first place? The answer Wesoky gives is this—the state wanted the ultimate success of the population policy; this led it to seek supplementary sources of funding from Ford and other foreign funds, and the state continued to keep its hand in the formulation and implementation of the Ford program itself. The political purpose is obvious in that the state attempted to justify itself in its population policy by showing that the state offers useful and safer means of introducing new population policies (Wesoky 2002, 211).

The "ethical principle" adopted at one of the conferences of the program is described as follows:

> Women are the major bearers of adverse consequences of overpopulation and the primary targets of population control programs. Their experiences should be considered, their voices be heard, and their participation be promoted in making decisions in reproduction and sexuality. (Program in Reproductive Health and Ethics 1994, p. 3, in Wesoky 2002, 211)

Obviously, this quote suggests the official Family Planning Program should be more compatible with women's autonomy and rights. I would like to dig deeper into this seeming compatibility.

Susan Greenhalgh wrote "Fresh Winds in Beijing: Chinese Feminists Speak Out on the One-Child Policy and Women's Lives."[6] She interviewed five prominent feminist scholars or activists including Liu Bohong, Qiu Renzong, Li Xiaojing and others. Both Liu and Qiu are involved in the program of women's Reproductive Health. Greenhalgh identifies three positions on state population policy among those interviewees, and Liu and Qiu are in the third position: overtly supporting the official narrative while quietly questioning parts of it (Greenhalgh, 865).

According to Greenhalgh, Liu cautiously explained that no one dared to oppose the birth-planning policy. Birth planning is the most important of China's basic policies. To openly challenge the government on this issue is to oppose the government, which is absolutely impermissible (867). Neither challenging nor endorsing the official line, Liu and Qiu remained implicitly critical while explicitly supportive of the party state's fundamental narrative of national policy. Both Liu and Qiu made it clear that the single biggest obstacle to the open discussion of these issues was political.

The interviews by Greenhalgh also noted the policy's different effects in rural and urban situations: While urban women have not been hurt and have in some ways even benefited from the one-child policy, rural women, especially those living in poor remote areas, have in many ways been harmed by the sharp restrictions on reproduction (869). Those women's voices are certainly hardly heard in experts' discussions about women's reproductive health.

Through Greenhalgh's discussion of the party's population policy in various reflections from Chinese feminist scholars, it is hard to see any compatible relationship between women's autonomy and rights and the government's top-down decision making. Women of certain groups have the chances to speak up, but not all women; certain topics or smaller issues regarding women's reproductive health might be permissible to discuss but no challenges can be made to the policy itself. But without a free discussion of the policy itself, the state's promise of centering women in the program of women's rights is just an empty pledge.

Cooperation between Chinese and Global Feminist Thinking

The third aspect I will discuss regarding a bottom-up democratic model is the impact of international ties between Chinese women scholars and activists and global norms of feminism. I hold a positive assessment of these necessary and productive exchanges on each side, especially the benefits the Chinese side appropriated from global communication. Nonetheless, I also see the blend of global feminist movements might prevent Chinese feminists from giving more attention to special Chinese women's problems, such as the gap between urban and rural women.

In the post-Mao era, an increasing member of exogenous forces have mobilized the Chinese women's movement. Because of the Fourth World Conference on Women and the Ford Foundation, ties with foreign activists have increased and in general Chinese women scholars and activists have become increasingly outward-looking (Wesoky 2002, 161). The Ford Foundation funding was specifically designed to increase both national and international women's networks and help Chinese women to attend NGO fora and activities. Through these ties, Chinese feminists have gained global perspectives on women's situations. A Chinese NGO activist made a comment:

> A difference between the Chinese and foreign women's movements is that China's has been done by the state, the Chinese movement is organized from top to bottom, and intellectuals don't participate in Fulian. The foreign is from bottom to top, with women consciously organizing, so these two ways have differences. (Wesoky 2002, 179)

According to Wesoky, this comment indicates the symbiotic social movement in current China that maintains a cooperative relationship with the state. This view also shows the value of women's empowerment in the global women's movement that will greatly influence Chinese feminists.

Chinese feminist thinkers and activists tried to catch up on discussions about international women's issues such as sexual harassment worldwide, domestic violence, marital rape, etc., which had not previously been given any attention by the state. Increasing attention to new issues has helped Chinese women find their voices and realize their collective problems such as subordinate sexual relations with men. The international norms enhanced Chinese women's definition of sexual oppression and how to end it, leading to a further challenging of the law. Zhang Xianyu notes: The main sufferers of sexual harassment are females, but our country's first comprehensive basic law defending women's rights and interests . . . has not yet stipulated this problem" (Zhang Xianyu 1995, 51). This is one of many indicators showing the great influence of learning from each other's experiences of sexual oppression in women's movements.

These positive international influences deepen feminist challenges to systematic male domination in Chinese society. However, these international ties are limited in their ability to include women's voices. To obtain information and funding from the Ford Foundation, one has to read and speak English and have a certain amount of spare time and skill to connect with foreigners. Only elite women (most of them are university women's studies scholars, NGO activists, Fulian women workers) have access to connections with international women and feminist activists, and therefore have their voices heard. Chinese working-class women and rural, poor women may have various issues and problems, yet their voices are weak, even mute. For instance, we have heard less about differences between rural and urban women's situations, about women's medical care in the countryside, about reproductive health for young women who are not married but abused by male partners, etc. A democratic model of women's equality should pay more attention to including these women's voices and interests because these women may be much worse off than the educated elite.

Empowerment of Chinese Women

A new democratic conception of equality for women includes a new concern for women's empowerment. Since Chinese culture and tradition have nurtured the strongest patriarchal social system and produced a powerful ideology to rationalize women's subordination, women's empowerment is particularly crucial. In this section, I start with the meaning of empowerment for women, then focus on how to empower women in the worst situations. In conclusion, I compare the idea of parity of effective voice (Jaggar 1998) with my model of democratic women's equality.

The Meaning of "Empowerment"

I would like to quote Feng Yuan, a journalist and women's scholar, who wrote an article in *Collection of Women's Studies*:

> The process of empowerment is individual and it also is collective. Because it is through participation in a group, it can cause women to organize, to adopt consciousness of and ability to act and promote changes to obtain full and constant development. Empowering women (fuquan funu), can be seen as a continuing process with several inherent interrelated and mutually reinforcing factors . . . Simply speaking, empowerment is a process that builds consciousness and ability, leads to even more equality, even greater influence on policy-making and decisions, and even greater transformative action. (Feng 1996)

Through this understanding of empowerment, consciousness and participation are important in seeking women's equality. Empowerment is the continuing process of developing women's sense of the value of democracy. I noted the collective aspect of such "empowerment"; this feature joins women with various identities: rural, urban, intellectual, working, old, young, all confronting diverse problems. One collective problem of rural, poor women, as I discussed in chapter 4, is the feminization of agriculture. The collective problem of working class women in urban districts is their being laid off from work. Young women in newly developing cities are facing serious workplace sexual harassment. To empower women in different situations requires multiple solutions.

Next, I will argue that the empowerment of rural, poor women requires state policy that favors these women. This is understandable if people are concerned with the special situation of these women in the current economic transformation.

Women's Empowerment Needs State Policy Favoring Women

As I discussed in chapter 4, women's status is declining in the economic transformation of the post-Mao period. However, the open-door policy of the party inevitably has brought in more democratic air and open-minded thinking on women's issues. International and national seminars, workshops, symposia, hotlines, etc., have raised deep questions about what kind of help women need. Women's self-consciousness and collective consciousness became more and more realized during and after the Fourth World Conference on Women, which took place in Beijing in 1995. However, feminists should consider not only the benefits of the state protecting women's rights, but also the costs. As we have seen, only the weak are supposed to need protection while the strong do not.

Accordingly, women are supposed to be weak by nature and are devalued by the implication of state protection. Thus, some female scholars suggest that the state should completely retreat from intervening in the economic transition and that women should fight for equality on their own. A few strong women have managed both career and household work successfully and become models of excellent contributors in economic development. Nevertheless, most women, especially women in poor, rural areas, are going backward through the "Feminization of Agriculture," and women in urban areas are forced back home for early retirement at middle age.

The argument that women should stay home, from the economic efficiency principle, is popular in today's Chinese male-dominant society, and Mao's call for women's equality in production is out of fashion. Should the state take more action to protect women's interests in the current economic transformation? As we saw in chapter 4, economic changes provided more benefits to men than to women, and feminization of agriculture emerged. Women will face more problems in the wake of economic globalization, especially after China's entry into the World Trade Organization (WTO). As three Chinese female experts on women's issues point out, although the WTO will bring Chinese women opportunities and development, they will face great risks and pay the price for greater integration into the global economy. They anticipate that women will have problems in employment, in health care, a decrease in pay during maternity leave, etc. Moreover, "With the decrease in value of farming product, women in rural areas will become poorer."[7]

Should the state continue to give women preferential treatment such as maternity leave with full pay and other benefits in women's health care? Should the state impose policies to request employers to hire a certain number of women in their enterprises such as establishing a law similar to the affirmative action law in the United States?

Peng Peiyun, president of the All China Women's Federation, comments that economic development will not naturally bring women's development and progress at the same pace. "So, necessary policies inclining to women should be adopted in order to gradually shrink the differences in development between the two sexes and to realize coordination and uniformity of economic benefit and social equality."[8] This is exactly what I suggest: the state should intervene in the justice and equity of social development in the current economic transition period.

Chinese women, particularly rural women in poor areas, deserve the state's special concern in changing their status quo. New state policies favoring women should not just copy Mao's policy (Mao promoted women's role in production but created problems such as double work days and balancing work and home), but focus on promoting women in a more fundamental way. The most important aspect of state policies must be how to promote women's voices. In order for women to be heard, women must participate in governmental decision-making in various jobs that traditionally have excluded them.

According to a survey conducted by the All China Women's Federation in 2000, "Chinese Women's Status in Transformation," the gender imbalance has grown in the last ten years compared with the first survey conducted in 1990. The number of laid-off women workers in state-owned enterprises was 18.9 percent higher than male laid-off workers. "Moreover, the income gap between women and men enlarged. Urban women's yearly income was 70.1 percent of men's, 7.4 percent lower than in 1990. Rural women's yearly income was just 59.6 percent of men's, where the gap widened, too."[9]

Nonetheless, according to the survey, gender equality is still moving into mainstream awareness for people in China. People believe gender equality was actually an ideal for the most part in Mao's time. "Now, having experienced the shock from the social transformation and hardships of life, women do not rely anymore on preferential treatment and special care; self-strength has become their need and pursuit in life" (*Women of China*/English Monthly, December 2001, 29-30). This view can be an objection to my above point that state policies must favor women and could also be a rationale for the state's retreat from intervening to lessen women's unemployment.

My first response to this view of women's self-reliance is to point to an important fact found in the survey. "[U]nder the environment of a market economy, there are signs of returning of the traditional ideas on division of labor based on sex."[10] This traditional mode of thinking is mainly a rehabilitation of Confucianism. Its emphasis on family values and women's proper roles advocates women's retreat from public roles. Hence, a popular viewpoint in recent years is: "Working well cannot equal marrying a good husband." Women accounted for 37.3 percent of those who approved of this viewpoint. This shows, according to the survey, that some young women still place hopes of changing their fate on men and marriage rather than on economic independence!

I completely agree with the idea of women's self-reliance, because it is the most important element in seeking their equality. Furthermore, we need to explore conditions to support it. However, unfortunately the current revival of the traditional view of women does not encourage women's self-reliance and independence. The social expectation and media also influence women's "choices" to be caregivers at home and to support their husbands' success. Beside these external reasons, women who believe in relying on a husband lack gender-consciousness. These women are not aware of the social phenomenon of *bao ernai* (keeping a second wife) and will easily become victims of rich men who are seeking the so-called "perfect life" that calls for more than one wife in one's so called "golden age." People should feel sorry for these new millionaires who value material pleasure more than the companionship of a good partner.

Obviously, cultural traditions and social expectations foster the idea of women's secondary position and promote their dependence on husbands. If the state really wants women to be independent and self-reliant, the state should create social conditions for women's equality by enacting policies that favor women in order to correct the historical discrimination against women.

The Chinese government is facing a dilemma regarding women's equality. On the one hand, most Chinese culture and tradition favors the idea of state solidarity and family stability, which requires women to sacrifice and play a complementary role to men. Because the policy decision-makers are overwhelmingly male, most of them are not immune to those traditions and accept the state's retreat, which neglects or even increases gender imbalance in the current market economy. On the other hand, Mao's policy of women's equality in production lasted three decades and effectively changed women's image and social position in people's mind. Most people thought that individual freedom and equality would be inevitable as China modernized.

Women should be treated as equal to men and their equality definitely needs the state's special care because women cannot fight against extremely obstinate patriarchy on their own. The male-centered culture would not allow or yield to women's equality; hence, the state should intervene to a certain degree to shrink the gender gap in the job market through laws against discrimination and policies to maintain gender balance.

Second, I am concerned that the state improve its policies favoring women. Remember that state interference in the economic changes and frequent residency checks made migrant women's situation worse, as we saw in chapter 4. The state has powers to limit people's preferences and to control migration labors in urban areas. In my view, the state should develop more effective policies and programs similar to "Double Learning" in the 1980s,[11] gender balance policies in the job market, and equality in girls' education, etc.

While the state takes care of women's special needs and interests, it should recognize the distinctions between *minben* and *minzhu*. Qi Liang, a Chinese professor of philosophy, makes the distinction between *minben* (representing people's interests) and *minzhu* (democracy): he argues that in three points the thought of *minben* fails to build a democratic politics in China. His first point is: *minben* (taking people's interests as the roots of ruling) is not *minzhu* (treating people with equal concern and respect). His second point is: the essence of *minben* gives absolute power to the ruler, not the ruled. The last point is: *minben* encourages a better and wiser ruler to take care of people's interests but offers no guarantee if he happens to be a tyrant; *minzhu* emphasizes people's equal rights and improves democratic politics with people's participation in ruling (Qi Liang 1998 and 1995).

Any policies built on the idea of *minben* are not sufficient to solve women's problems, because the state policies and caring for women's interests can only create preconditions for women's seeking equality. Women also need a democratic social environment to express their issues. Only when the idea of *minzhu* (democracy) takes place in women's issues can women's equality progress toward its full accomplishment. And this accomplishment definitely requires women's self-direction, self-reliance, and self-fulfillment.

My third response to the issue of state policies is the issue of developing a democratic methodology for favoring women as China moves toward gender equality. Since state policies are inclined toward the paternalistic control of women's minds, such as how Mao's class expansion subjected every issue to class analysis and silenced women's voices, a democratic method is necessary to replace paternalistic thinking. This means that women should be involved in policy decision-making, in observing the implementation of policy programs, and in adjusting and solving problems in the practice of gender equality. Women should be the subjects of seeking women's equality, not just objects of state policies. Women should have a say about what kind of equality they want and what policies can really help them reach the goal of gender balance and equality. Until women have political representatives, who strive for women's equality at the top decision-making level, state policies with a democratic style must continue to help women get an equal footing with men.

Parity of Effective Voice and Women's Empowerment

The previous models of sexual equality I discussed consider separate issues of political, moral, and economic gender inequality and lack a comprehensive understanding of the larger framework of women's subordination. My new conception of democratic equality for Chinese women should focus on this framework. This model will be compatible with the idea of "parity of effective voice" explicitly proposed in the article "Sexual Equality as Parity of Effective Voice" (Jaggar 1998). Making women's voices equally effective to men's at a policy decision-making level and giving them public recognition is the new model's goal. I will briefly explain the meaning of women's effective voice, then compare this idea with Chinese women's current situation, and finally summarize the significance of the new model.

Alison Jaggar argues that parity of effective voice requires that all women (not only the most privileged) should be able to express their specific interests and concerns. This, in return, requires that they must challenge the ways in which women as a whole and as a specific group have been culturally and symbolically disregarded and devalued. Women must redefine and reclaim themselves as members of a distinct group with legitimate interests. Jaggar describes women's voices as follows:

> Developing women's "authentic" voice requires that women come to regard themselves collectively as sources of distinct and valid perceptions and insights. In other words, women must claim a collective

moral and epistemic authority and they must claim it not in spite of
but in virtue of their collective identities as women. (1998, 190)

Why must women claim a collective moral and epistemic authority that
highlights their collective identities as women? First, it is hard to hear women's
voices because of what L. Thomas calls "their categorical diminishing." For
example, the voices of farming women in the poor and rural areas are rarely
taken seriously as significant concerns. Even though there have been women's
voices, these voices are not as effective as men's. Why are women's voices diminished in public recognition? Jaggar adopts Thomas's idea of a diminished
social category:

> Just as a person does not know what it is like to be a bat by hanging
> upside down with closed eyes, [so] a person does not know what it is
> like to be a member of a diminished social category merely on ac-
> count of having been affronted and insulted by a diminished social
> category person. (Jaggar 1998, 196; Thomas, *supra* note 16, at 240)

The argument goes, since persons from privileged social classes have no
"vantage point" to grasp the morally significant experiences of people in diminished social categories, they should accord those speakers "moral deference."
"[M]oral deference may be viewed as a kind of discursive affirmative action,"
and it "assumes that people from privileged social classes may educate their
emotions so that they become capable of sensitive moral perception and judg-
ment." Through practicing moral deference, people can learn to bear witness to
the moral pain of those who have suffered oppression. In addition to practicing
moral deference and being sensitive to women's suffering, listeners should defer
to women's moral authority as members of a group that has distinctive experiences and perceptions. Only by these two conditions, "Women must be accorded
recognition not as genderless humans but as a collective source of distinctive
perceptions and insights—insights made possible by their specific gendered social locations" (Jaggar 1998, 196-97).

The other aspect of parity of effective voice is how to make women's voices
effective. First, listeners must note that women's experiences are shaped, inter-
preted, and assigned meaning through public opinion, so individual women's
experiences can be viewed in light of women's specific collective identities as
subjects of common experiences. "Thus, when a speaker is accorded moral authority in virtue of her collective identity, she should be heard as saying something not only about her own life but also about the lives of others who share
that identity" (Jaggar 1998, 197). Therefore, personal narratives of individuals
from subordinated or stigmatized groups have implications beyond the personal;
they have broader social significance.

Recognizing women's collective moral authority commits listeners to taking women's voices seriously, which implies critically accepting women's per-

spectives on prevailing practices and norms, including conceptions of sexual equality. The public recognition necessary for women's voices to be developed and heard must include multidimensional recognition. Cultural recognition is not independent of economic and political recognition—they are combined in people's social lives. Thus, Jaggar claims: "In order to ensure that their voices are effective, women also need social power, including recognized credentials, institutional positions, and material resources" (1998, 199). Such recognition of multiple dimensions includes but goes beyond the formal political system.

The parity of effective voice for women needs not only moral recognition and moral deference but also requires a degree of substantive material equality (Jaggar 1998, 200). Thus, the necessary and sufficient conditions for parity of effective voice for women are inseparable pursuits of political, cultural, and economic recognition, for social power, equality, and material equality between genders.

The model of parity of effective voice for women explicitly presents how a democratic conception of sex equality needs to formulate and articulate its content. The theory of parity of effective voice also applies to my suggestion that the Chinese state favor women in the current economic transformation. Chinese women need available a language and location to express their specific needs, such as various NGO fora. On the other hand, the state officials and people who care for women's equality, as listeners to women's voices, should make great efforts to get women's voices publicly recognized through their practice of moral deference and endowing women with moral authority as the collective identity of a specific group. Hearing and making women's voices effective are concrete conditions in practicing a democratic model of seeking women's equality, and these two conditions are crucial in empowering Chinese women for self-motivated equality.

Since taking women's voices seriously does not mean accepting them uncritically (not all women are feminist supporters and some of them may favor a traditional view of women), listeners to women's voices for the purpose of eliminating female oppression must consider women as the collective moral authority of their specific group. Women's concrete situations differ: women are farming in the poor villages; women are unemployed in their middle forties; women are living as second wives with rich partners, etc. These specific groups of women should have an authentic language for their experiences and receive public recognition of their subordinated positions. Recognizing these women's speech and taking their voices seriously can start to change their unfair positions and promote their equality.

Some might object to applying the idea of parity of effective voice to the current Chinese women's situation. The three aspects—finding women's voices, hearing women's voices, and making their voices equally effective to men's—are too demanding for a third world country like China. Someone will argue that it is too idealistic for women in China because more than half of them hardly

read, much less strive for their formal rights. The current Chinese feminist challenges are too weak to confront the revival of Confucianism with its old version
of care ethics, the fast economic changes with their emphasis on economic efficiency, and people's fatigue with the frequent political struggles of Mao's reign.

Nevertheless, I will respond, there is no reason for feminists to stop striving
for women's equality in China, though the cause has been very complicated and
arduous. I believe the new conception of democratic sexual equality focusing on
parity of effective voice will direct the Chinese women's cause toward its right-
ful development of equality, freedom, and full emancipation. Because the cause
of equality needs multidimensional attention and public recognition of women's
specific oppression, it will be a long and complex process rather than a once-
and-for-all revolutionary movement.

Considering the hardship and long-term struggle of seeking Chinese
women's equality in a society with such a tradition of gender inequality, I am
not so optimistic as to merely rely on fine theories of sexual equality: Chinese
women will face tremendous obstacles in their pursuit of gender fairness and
equality. But I firmly believe that only the democratic model of women's equality can guide women in the right direction toward women's (and men's) full
emancipation and human happiness.

At the end of this section, I would like to suggest concretely what Chinese
feminists should do to empower women in promoting women's positions and
ending women's sufferings step by step.

First, all Chinese NGOs and the government need to cooperatively empower women by encouraging them to develop their own authentic language and
different voices. Together, NGOs and the state should develop an autonomous
women's movement by funding and organizing all channels for making all
voices, especially disadvantaged women's voices, effective at the decision-
making level.

Second, programs in women's studies urgently need to consider women's
situations (especially in rural districts) under the current economic changes and
the globalization of the Chinese economy (e.g., via the WTO), the impact of the
traditional culture on women's situations, and the conflicts between women's
self-sacrifice for the family and personal self-fulfillment. Women's development
in seeking equality must be multidimensional—political, moral, economic,
etc.—addressing multiple concerns rather than a separate single solution.

Third, dialogues and idea exchanges between different perspectives of
global feminist thinking certainly help Chinese women's pursuit of equality.
This learning and exchanging must be based on the principle of cooperation
rather than domination. The field construction of feminist scholarship in China
is an urgent task as a part of constructing a global feminist cause against all
oppression and particularly women's oppression.

Conclusion

To summarize this project, I examined four models of sexual equality. The three models of formal equality, substantive equality, and equal opportunity failed to promote Chinese women's self-directed consciousness for a full emancipation and equality. The common problem of these models is their lack of focus on women's collective consciousness as an oppressed sex class and on how the sexist society consolidated women's oppression by keeping them silent and sacrificed. The new model of democratic sexual equality stresses the empowerment of women through the cooperation of various Chinese NGOs and the government through bottom-up rather than top-down state policies. This sounds like a conflicting strategy because the state policy is seen as top-down. Nevertheless, this is the only possible way to make cooperation with the state, which has officially supported gender equality from Mao to post-Mao leaders, for the purpose of pushing women's cause toward a full sexual equality. Only a democratic framework can do a better job to improve Chinese women's situations and enable women's self-motivated liberation and equality.

Notes

1. See the debate, Jay Gallagher, "Do Muscles Matter?" and Xinyan Jiang, "Reply to Jay Gallagher," *Hypatia* (Winter 2002) 53-70; 71-76.
2. The Confucian golden rule for reciprocity is written in Confucius's *The Analects* (Book VII: 2): Do not impose on others what you yourself do not desire. See David S. Nivison (1996), 59-76.
3. Dewey was called the "Second Confucius" during his twenty-six-month visit in China beginning on May 1, 1919. But he was condemned as an expression of Western imperialism after the establishment of the People's Republic of China, and a purge of Deweyan pragmatism was begun. See Ames and Hall (1999), 141.
4. See Qi Liang, *Qi Liang Ji* (*SiXiangZheWenCong*) (Shanghai: Xuelin Publisher, 1998), 105-14; *Critiques of Neo Confucianism* (*Xin ru xue pi pan*) (Shanghai: Sanlian Shuku 1995), 429-40.
5. See Sharon Wesoky, *Chinese Feminism Faces Globalization* (New York: Routledge, 2002).
6. Susan Greenhalgh, "Fresh Winds in Beijing: Chinese Feminists Speak Out on the One-Child Policy and Women's Lives," *Signs* (Spring 2001), 847-86.
7. See Wang Xiaoming, "WTO a Monster or an Angel for Chinese Women?" *Women of China*/English Monthly, December 2000, 24-25.
8. See Fu Yansuo, "The Survey: Chinese Women's Status in Transformation," *Women of China*/English Monthly, December 2001, 30.
9. *Women of China*/English Monthly, December 2001, 29.
10. *Women of China*/English Monthly, December 2001, 30.

11. "Double Learning and Double Competing" is a nationwide program run by the All China Women's Federation in collaboration with other government organizations since 1989. The project targets rural women, and its aims are to help them learn to read and write, learn skills and technology, and compete for contributions to production. See Zhang Xiaoquan (1999), 57-58.

Selected Bibliography

All China Women's Federation (ACWF), Unit of History of Women's Movement. *Wusi Shiqi FunuWenti Wenxuan* (*Selected Writings on Women's Issues during the May Fourth Period*). Beijing: Shenghuo Dushu Xinzhi Sanlian Shudian, 1981.

All China Women's Federation (ACWF). *Mao Zedong, Zhou Enlai, Liu Shaoqi, and Zhu De on Women's Liberation.* Beijing: People's Press, 1988.

All China Women's Federation (ACWF), ed. *Important Documents of Chinese Women's Movement.* Beijing: People's Press, 1979.

Ames, Roger T., and David Hall. *Thinking from the Han: Self, Truth, and Transcendence in Chinese and Western Culture.* Albany: State University of New York Press, 1998.

Ames, Roger T., and David Hall. *The Democracy of the Dead: Dewey, Confucius, and The Hope for Democracy in China.* Chicago: Open Court, 1999.

Avakian, Bob. *Mao Tsetung: Immortal Contribution.* Chicago: RCP Publications, 1979.

Ban, Zhao. *NuJie (Admonitions for Women).* Beijing: Zhongyang Minzu Daixu Chuban She (Central Nationality University Press), 1996.

Bartke, Wolfgang. *Who's Who in the People's Republic of China.* New York: M.E. Sharpe, 1991.

Bingham, Marjorie Wall, and Susan Hill Gross. *Women in Modern China: Transition, Revolution, and Contemporary Times.* St. Louis Park, MN: Glenhurst Publications, 1980.

Chan, Wing-tsit. *A Source Book in Chinese Philosophy.* Princeton, NJ: Princeton University Press, 1963.

Chen, Muhua. "The Whole World's Women Unite for Striving to Realize Equality, Development, and Peace." *QiuShi* (*Seeking Truth*), in *Women's Studies: Information from the Press* (1994): 15-17.

Chodorow, Nancy. *The Reproduction of Mothering.* Berkeley: University of California Press, 1978.

Chow, Kai-wing. *The Rise of Confucian Ritualism in Late Imperial China.* Stanford, CA: Stanford University Press, 1994.

Croll, Elisabeth. *Feminism and Socialism in China.* Boston: Routledge, 1978.

Cunningham, Frank. *Theories of Democracy: A Critical Introduction.* London: Routledge, 2002.

Engels, Frederick. *The Origin of the Family, Private Property, and the State.* New York: International Publishers, 1993.

Fang, Li-tian. *Zhongguo Gudai Zhexue Wenti Fazhan Shi* (*The Development of Philoso-*

phical Issues in Ancient China). Beijing: Zhonghua Shuju (China Book Bureau), 1990.

Fei, Xiaotong. *From the Soil: The Foundations of Chinese Society, A Translation of Fei Xiaotong's Xiangtu Zhongguo.* Berkeley: University of California Press, 1992.

Feng, Yu-lan. *A Short History of Chinese Philosophy.* New York: The Macmillan Company, 1948.

Feng, Yuan. "Women's Empowerment." In *Funu Yanjiu Luncong* (*Collection of Women's Studies* 1996) 17: 57-58.

Ferguson, Ann. *Sexual Democracy: Women, Oppression, and Revolution.* Boulder, CO: Westview Press, 1991.

Fingarette, Herbert. *Confucius: The Secular as Sacred.* New York: Harper and Row, 1972.

Gallagher, Jay. "Do Muscles Matter?" *Hypatia: A Journal of Feminist Philosophy* 17, no. 1 (2002): 53-70.

Gao, Xiaoxian. "The Transition of Labors in Rural China and the Trend of Feminization of Agriculture." *Studies of Sociology*, February 1994.

Gilmartin, Christina Kelley. *Engendering the Chinese Revolution: Radical Women, Communist Politics, and Mass Movements in the 1920s.* Berkeley: University of California Press, 1995.

Greenhalgh, Susan. "Fresh Winds in Beijing: Chinese Feminists Speak Out on the One-Child Policy and Women's Lives." *Signs* 26, no. 3 (Spring 2001): 847-86.

Hartmann, Heidi. "The Unhappy Marriage of Marxism and Feminism." Pp. 1-42 in *Women and Revolution*, edited by Lydia Sargent. Boston: South End Press, 1981.

He, Qinglian. "Analysis of Social Changes of Women's Status in Contemporary China." *Dangdai Zhongguo Yanjiu* (*Modern China Studies*) 2 (2001).

Hemmel, Vibeke. *Women in Rural China: Policy Towards Women Before and After the Cultural Revolution.* Atlantic Highlands, NJ: Humanities Press, 1984.

Hu, Shi. *The Chinese Renaissance: The Haskell Lectures 1933.* New York: Paragon Book Reprint Corp., 1963.

Hu, Shi. *Collections of Writings of Hu Shi, Series 6: On Issues of Chastity.* Hong Kong: Hong Kong Yuanliu Press, 1986.

Huang, Pumin. *Dong Zhong-shu yu Xin Ruxue* (*Tung Chung-shu and Neo-Confucianism*). Taibei: Wen Jin Press, 1992.

Huang, Xiyi. "Divided Gender, Divided Women: State Policy and the Labor Market." Pp. 90-107 in *Women of China: Economic and Social Transformation*, edited by Jackie West. New York: St. Martin's Press, 1999.

Hunan Women Federation, ed. *Funuxuegailun* (*Introduction to Women Studies*). Changsha: Huan Press, 1987.

Jaggar, Alison M. *Feminist Politics and Human Nature.* Totowa, NJ: Rowman & Littlefield Publishers, 1983.

Jaggar, Alison M. "Affirmative Action, Sex Equality, and Meritocratic Justice in the United States." In *Quoten Und Gleichstellung Von Frau Und Mann* (Separatum/unverkauflicher Sonderdruck 1995a): 71-108.

Jaggar, Alison M. "Caring as a Feminist Practice of Moral Reason." Pp. 230-50 in *Justice and Care: Essential Readings in Feminist Ethics*, edited by Virginia Held. Boulder, CO: Westview Press, 1995b.

Jaggar, Alison M. "Sexual Equality as Parity of Effective Voice." *Journal of Contemporary Legal Issues* (Spring 1998): 179-202.

Jiang, Xinyan. "The Dilemma Faced by Chinese Feminists." *Hypatia: A Journal of Feminist Philosophy* 15, no. 3 (2002): 140-60.

Jiang, Xinyan. "Reply to Jay Gallagher." *Hypatia: A Journal of Feminist Philosophy* 17, no. 1 (2002): 71-76.

Jin, Yihong. "Cultural Critique of Violence against Women in Family." *Expert Workshop On Fighting Domestic Violence Against Women: Social, Ethical, and Legal Issues*. Beijing, 1997.

Kam, Louie. *Critiques of Confucius in Contemporary China*. Hong Kong: The Chinese University of Hong Kong, 1998.

Koggel, Christine M. *Perspectives on Equality: Constructing a Relational Theory*. Lanham, MD: Rowman & Littlefield Publishers, 1998.

Lau, D. C. *Confucius: The Analects*. New York: Penguin Group, 1979.

Lee, Lily Xiao Hong. *The Virtue of Yin: Studies on Chinese Women*. Australia: Wild Peony, 1994.

Lee, Pauline. "Li Zhi and John Stuart Mill: A Confucian Feminist Critique of Liberal Feminism." Pp. 113-32 in *The Sage and the Second Sex: Confucianism, Ethics, and Gender*, edited by Chenyang Li. Chicago: Open Court Press, 2000.

Li, Chenyang. "The Confucian Concept of *Jen* and Feminist Ethics of Care: A Comparative Study." *Hypatia* 9, no. 1 (1994): 70-89.

Li, Chenyang. *The Tao Encounters the West: Explorations in Comparative Philosophy*. Albany: State University of New York Press, 1999.

Li, Chenyang, ed. *The Sage and the Second Sex: Confucianism, Ethics, and Gender*. Chicago: Open Court Press, 2000.

Li, Dun. *Expert Workshop On Fighting Domestic Violence Against Women: Social, Ethical, and Legal Issues*. Beijing: Sanlian Bookstore, 1997a.

Li, Dun. "Marital Rape In China." Pp. 325-45 in *Equality and Development: Studies of Gender and China*, vol. 2, edited by Xiaojiang Li. Beijing: Sanlian Bookstore, 1997b.

Li, Jingzhi. "A View On the Conflicts of Women's Identities and Strategies for Resolution in Theory." Pp. 226-30 in *Jiaose De Kunhuo Yu Nuren De Chulu* (*The Puzzle of Identities and Opportunities of Women*), edited by Tong Shaosu. Hangzhou: Zhejiang People Press, 1995.

Li, Jun, ed. *Wu Jing Quan Yi: LiJi Quan Yi* (*Interpretations of Five Classics: Interpretation of the Book of Rites*), vol. 2. Chang Chun: Chang Chun Press, 1980.

Li, Xiaojiang. *Eve's Transcending: A Theoretical Outline of Women's Studies in China*. Zhengzhou: Henan People's Press, 1988.

Li, Xiaojiang. *Women's Hope for the Future*. Liaoning: Liaoning People's Press, 1989.

Li, Xiaojiang. "Creating a Space for Women: Women's Studies in China in the 1980s." *Signs* 20, no. 1 (Autumn 1994): 137-51.

Li, Xiaojiang. *Pingdeng Yu Fazhan* (*Equality and Development: Studies of Gender and China*), vol. 2. Beijing: Sanlian Bookstore, 1997.

Li, Ze-hou. *Zhongguo Gudai Sixiang Shi Lun (On the History of Ancient Chinese Thought)*. Taibei: Feng Yun Shi Dai Press, 1990.

Lin, Chun. "Gender Equality in China: Between the State and the Market." Pp. 48-61 in *International Symposium: Chinese Women and Feminist Thought*. Beijing, Grand View Garden Hotel. June 21-24, 1995.

Lin, Chun, Liu Bohong, and Jin Yihong. "China." Pp. 108-17 in *A Companion to Feminist Philosophy*, edited by Alison M. Jaggar and Iris Marion Young. Oxford, UK: Blackwell Publishers, 2000.

Liu, Chao. "Safeguarding Women's Interests." *Peking Review* (March 1974).

Louie, Kam. *Critiques of Confucius in Contemporary China*. New York: St. Martin's Press, 1980.

Luo, Suwen. *Nuxing Yu Jindai Zhongguo Shehui (Female Gender and Modern Chinese Society)*. Shanghai: Shanghai People Press, 1996.

MacKinnon, Catharine A. *Feminism Unmodified: Discourses on Life and Law*. Cambridge, MA: Harvard University Press, 1987.

Mao, Zedong. *Quotations From Chairman Mao*. Peking: Foreign Language Press, 1966.

Mao, Zedong. *Selected Works of Mao Tse-tung*. 4 vols. Beijing: Foreign Language Press, 1967.

Mao, Zedong. *Early Writings of Mao Zedong, 1912.6-1920.11*. Beijing: Internal Press, 1990.

Mill, John Stuart. *The Subjection of Women*. Edited by Sue Mansfield. Arlington Heights, Il: Harlan Davidson, Inc., 1980.

Minow, Martha. *Making All the Difference: Inclusion, Exclusion, and American Law*. Ithaca, NY: Cornell University Press, 1990.

Nivison, David S. *The Ways of Confucianism: Investigations in Chinese Philosophy*. Edited by Bryan W. Van Norden. Chicago: Open Court, 1996.

Pan, Suimin. "Why Is It Difficult to Make A Definition of Marital Rape?" Pp. 85-86 in *Expert Workshop On Fighting Domestic Violence Against Women: Social, Ethical, and Legal Issues*. Beijing: Sanlian Bookstore, 1997.

Renmin Rebao (People's Daily) (Beijing). "Let All Women Rise Up." Editorial, March 8, 1974.

Perkins, Dorothy. *Encyclopedia of China: The Essential Reference to China, Its History and Culture*. New York: Round Table Press, 1999.

Qi, Liang. *Critiques of Neo-Confucianism (Xin ru xue pi pan)*. Shanghai: Sanlian Shuku, 1995.

Qi, Liang. *Qi Liang Ji (SiXiangZheWenCong)*. Shanghai, China: Xuelin Publisher, 1998.

Raphals, Lisa. *Sharing the Light: Representations of Women and Virtue in Early China*. Albany: State University of New York Press, 1998.

Rhode, Deborah. L., ed. *Theoretical Perspectives On Sexual Difference*. Binghamton, New York: Yale University Press, 1997.

Robinson, Fiona. *Globalizing Care: Ethics, Feminist Theory, and International Relations*. Boulder, CO: Westview Press, 1999.

Rosemont, Henry. "Classical Confucian and Contemporary Feminist Perspectives On the Self: Some Parallels and Their Implications." Pp. 63-82 in *Culture and Self: Philoso-*

phical and Religious Perspectives, East and West, edited by Douglas Allen. Boulder, CO: Westview Press, 1997.

Routledge. *Concise Routledge Encyclopedia of Philosophy.* New York: Routledge, 2000.

Rubin, Gayle. "The Traffic in Women: Notes on the 'Political Economy' of Sex." Pp. 27-62 in *The Second Wave: A Reader in Feminist Theory,* edited by Linda Nicholson. New York: Routledge, 1997.

Russell, Bertrand. *Marriage and Morals.* New York: Liveright Publishing, 1929.

Sargent, Lydia, ed. *Women and Revolution: A Discussion of the Unhappy Marriage Of Marxism and Feminism.* Montreal: Black Rose Books, 1981.

Schram, Stuart. *The Thought of Mao Tse-Tung.* Cambridge: Cambridge University Press, 1989.

Shaanxi Province Women's Federation, ed. *Statistics On Chinese Women (1949-1989).* Beijing: China Statistical Publishing, 1990.

Shanley, Mary Lyndon and Carole Pateman, eds. *Feminist Interpretations and Political Theory.* University Park, PA: The Pennsylvania State University Press, 1991.

Snow, Edward. *Red Star Over China.* Hebei: Hebei People Press, 1992.

Song, Lina. "The Role of Women in Labor Migration: A Case Study in Northern China." Pp. 69-89 in *Women of China: Economic and Social Transformation,* edited by Jackie West. New York: St. Martin's Press, 1999.

Spelman, Elizabeth V. *Inessential Women: Problems of Exclusion in Feminist Thought.* Boston: Beacon Press, 1988.

Sun, Loying, and Lu Lifen. *Xuexi Yu Pipan (Study and Criticism)* (January 10, 1975).

Tan, Shen. "Women in China: Problems for Analysis: Two Major Women Issues Emerging in the Reform of Today's China." Pp. 161-72 in *International Symposium: Chinese Women and Feminist Thought.* Beijing, June 21-24, 1995.

Tang, Zongli, and Zuo, Bing. *Maoism and Chinese Culture.* Commack, NY: Nova Science, 1996.

Tian, Jia-ying. *Zhongguo Funu Shenghuo Shihua (Discourse on the History of Chinese Women's Life).* Beijing: China Women Press, 1982.

Tong, Shaosu, ed. *Jiaose de Kunhuo yu Nuren de Chulu (The Puzzle of Identities and Opportunities of Women).* Hangzhou: Zhejiang People Press, 1995.

Trebilcot, Joyce. "Sex Roles." Pp. 40-48 in *"Femininity,""Masculinity,"and "Androgyny": A Modern Philosophical Discussion,* edited by Mary Vetterling-Braggin. Totowa, NJ: Littlefield, Adams & Co. 1982.

Tu, Weiming. *Confucian Thought: Selfhood as Creative Transformation.* Albany: State University of New York Press, 1985.

Waley, Arthur. *The Analects of Confucius.* New York: Random House, 1938.

Wang, Qi. "State-Society Relations and Women's Political Participation." Pp. 19-44 in *Women of China: Economic and Social Transformation,* edited by Jackie West. New York: St. Martin's Press, 1999.

Wang, Xingjuan."The Family Role of Women in Leadership." In *The Puzzle of Identities and Opportunities of Women,* edited by Tong Shaosu. Hangzhou: Zhejiang People Press, 1995a.

Wang, Xingjuan. "Two Breakthroughs of the Notion of Self of Contemporary Chinese Women." Pp. 197-98 in *International Symposium: Chinese Women and Feminist Thought.* Beijing, June 21-24, 1995b.

Wang, Zheng. *Women in The Chinese Enlightenment: Oral and Textual Histories.* Berkeley: University of California Press, 1999.

Wei, Ying-min. *A New Evaluation On Mao's Ethic Thinking.* Beijing: Beijing University 1993.

Wesoky, Sharon. *Chinese Feminism Faces Globalization.* New York: Routledge, 2002.

Wolf, Margery. *Revolution Postponed: Women in Contemporary China.* Stanford, CA: Stanford University Press, 1985.

Wolf, Margery. "Beyond the Patrilineal Self: Constructing Gender in China." Pp. 251-68 in *Self as Person in Asian Theory and Practice,* edited by Roger Ames and David Hall. Albany: State University of New York Press, 1994.

Wolf, Margery, and Roxane Witke, eds. *Women in Chinese Society.* Stanford, CA: Stanford University Press, 1975.

Women of China/English Monthly, December 2000.

Women of China/English Monthly, December 2001.

Wonack, Brantly. *The Foundation of Mao Zedong's Political Thought 1917-1935.* Honolulu: The University Press of Hawaii, 1982.

Xiang, Zi. "In Men's Eyes: Women Who Participate in and Take Part in Discussion, Politics, and Government." Pp. 91-96 in *Chinese Law and Government: Women and Politics in China (1),* 26, no. 6 (November-December 1993).

Xu, Anqi. "The Origins of Domestic Violence in Cities." Pp. 262-75 in *Equality and Development: Studies of Gender and China,* vol. 2, edited by Li Xiaojiang. Beijing: Sanlian Bookstore, 1997.

Xu, Quan-xing. *Mao Ze-dong's Late Theory and Practice (1956-1976).* Beijing: Great Encyclopedia Publishers, 1995.

Yang, Bojun. *Lunyu Yizhu (Interpretation of Analects).* Beijing: Zhonghua Shuju (China Book Bureau), 1996.

Yang, Chungui, and Li Huolin. *Mao Zedong as a Philosopher.* Beijing: The Party's School Press, 1994.

Young, Marilyn B., ed. *Women in China: Studies in Social Change and Feminism.* Ann Arbor: Center for Chinese Studies, the University of Michigan, 1973.

Yuan, Lijun. "Ethics of Care and Concept of *Jen*: A Reply to Chenyang Li." *Hypatia: A Journal of Feminist Philosophy* 17, no. 1 (2002): 107-29.

Zhang, Xianyu. "What to Do when Facing Sexual Harassment." *Hunyin yu Jiating (Marriage and Family)* (August 1995): 50-51.

Zhang, Xiaoquan Heather. "Understanding Changes in Women's Status in the Context of the Recent Rural Reform." Pp. 45-68 in *Women of China: Economic and Social Transformation,* edited by Jackie West. New York: St. Martin's Press, 1999.

Zhang, Hao. "The Critique and Affirmation of the May Fourth Movement." Pp. 65-91 in *Cong Wusi Dao Xin Wusi (From May Fourth to the New May Fourth: Cultural China Supplement 1),* edited by Yangshan Zhou. Taibei: Shibao Wenhua Chuban Qiye Youxiangongsi, 1989.

Zhao, X. "Rural Chinese Women: Getting Rid of Illiteracy and Receiving Technical Training." *People's Daily* (overseas edition) (November 22, 1994): 3.

Zheng, Yefu. *DaiJia Lun: Yige Shehuixue de Xinshijiao* (*On Prices: A New Perspective from Sociology*). Beijing: Sanlian Bookstore, 1995.

Zhou, Yangshan, ed. *Cong Wusi Dao Xin Wusi* (*From May Fourth to the New May Fourth; Cultural China Supplement 1*). Taibei: Shibao Wenhua Chuban Qiye Youxian gongsi, 1989.

Index

About the Author

Lijun Yuan received her Master's in philosophy at Nankai University, China, in 1982 and became an associate professor at the Philosophy Institute, Beijing Academy of Social Sciences, in 1992. One of her publications in Chinese is the translation of Bertrand Russell's book *Logic and Knowledge* (1996). She came to the University of Colorado at Boulder to study feminist philosophy and earned her Ph.D. in philosophy in 2002. Her main focus has been on feminist ethics with a particular emphasis on comparing Chinese and Western feminist philosophies on issues of women's equality. She published her article "Ethics of Care and Concept of *Jen*" (*Hypatia: A Journal of Feminist Philosophy*, Winter 2002) and has had several publications in philosophy and women's issues in Chinese.

Dr. Yuan has taught ethics, contemporary moral issues, Asian philosophy, and critical thinking at the University of Colorado at Boulder, California State University, Fresno, and Texas State University-San Marcos. In spring 2005 she created an honors course, *The Ethics of Care: East and West*, in the honors program at Texas State University-San Marcos, where she holds a tenure track position.